Michael Acton

ITIL: A Decision & Implementation Strategy for US Government Agencies

Michael Acton

ITIL: A Decision & Implementation Strategy for US Government Agencies

LAP LAMBERT Academic Publishing

Impressum / Imprint

Bibliografische Information der Deutschen Nationalbibliothek: Die Deutsche Nationalbibliothek verzeichnet diese Publikation in der Deutschen Nationalbibliografie; detaillierte bibliografische Daten sind im Internet über http://dnb.d-nb.de abrufbar.
Alle in diesem Buch genannten Marken und Produktnamen unterliegen warenzeichen-, marken- oder patentrechtlichem Schutz bzw. sind Warenzeichen oder eingetragene Warenzeichen der jeweiligen Inhaber. Die Wiedergabe von Marken, Produktnamen, Gebrauchsnamen, Handelsnamen, Warenbezeichnungen u.s.w. in diesem Werk berechtigt auch ohne besondere Kennzeichnung nicht zu der Annahme, dass solche Namen im Sinne der Warenzeichen- und Markenschutzgesetzgebung als frei zu betrachten wären und daher von jedermann benutzt werden dürften.

Bibliographic information published by the Deutsche Nationalbibliothek: The Deutsche Nationalbibliothek lists this publication in the Deutsche Nationalbibliografie; detailed bibliographic data are available in the Internet at http://dnb.d-nb.de.
Any brand names and product names mentioned in this book are subject to trademark, brand or patent protection and are trademarks or registered trademarks of their respective holders. The use of brand names, product names, common names, trade names, product descriptions etc. even without a particular marking in this works is in no way to be construed to mean that such names may be regarded as unrestricted in respect of trademark and brand protection legislation and could thus be used by anyone.

Coverbild / Cover image: www.ingimage.com

Verlag / Publisher:
LAP LAMBERT Academic Publishing
ist ein Imprint der / is a trademark of
AV Akademikerverlag GmbH & Co. KG
Heinrich-Böcking-Str. 6-8, 66121 Saarbrücken, Deutschland / Germany
Email: info@lap-publishing.com

Herstellung: siehe letzte Seite /
Printed at: see last page
ISBN: 978-3-659-43677-2

Zugl. / Approved by: Diamond Bar, California Intercontinental University, Diss., 2012

ITIL: A Decision & Implementation Strategy for US Government Agencies

By Dr. Michael C. Acton

Contents

List of Tables and Figures

Foundational Issues in Implementing ITIL within a U. S. government agency

Since the late 1980's when the concepts that were to be known as Information Technology Infrastructure Library (ITIL) were first introduced, organizations have realized the benefits of a standardized framework, but many organizations are unable to find a way to incorporate this framework into their day to day operational business processes. Since ITIL covers such a breadth and depth of IT services, and because it takes an academic slant, it is often regarded by IT practitioners as overly cumbersome to implement. The ITIL framework is also sometimes regarded as too generic to be useful for off-the-shelf usage and implementation (Baschab, Piot, & Carr, 2007). These concerns need not prevent an organization from utilizing ITIL best practices and this book will illustrate how this can be accomplished within a U. S. government organization.

Many organizations struggle with developing a working methodology for implementing Information Technology Infrastructure Library best practice within their organizations. The problem for the United States (U.S.) government agency which desires to adopt this practice is the existing ITIL implementation guidance fails to address a U.S. government agency's unique challenges of reduced federal budgets, lack of qualified employees, and added regulatory constraints. Often it is the government agency leadership that will dictate how ITIL will be implemented. This often entails selecting a "low hanging fruit" ITIL process to implement; not fully understanding that although easiest to implement, may not yield the greatest benefit to the agency based on resources expended.

What is missing in the available ITIL implementation guidance is a linkage between the agencies' strategy and vision to the critical tasks being performed by their employees. An ability to align the strategy, vision, and critical tasks to an associated ITIL process can provide the agency insight into a more cost effective implementation strategy. An ability to do this will be critical to any government agency faced with reduced budgets and the challenge of "doing more with less."

Without a full understanding of the basics of ITIL it would be impossible to understand how best to utilize the methodology in any organizational setting. To this end, an understanding of the history and all processes and functions of ITIL are needed. This will be discussed in some detail to lay the foundation to adequately address the problem mentioned previously. A discussion of ITIL's inception in the early 1980s to its current Version 3 approach is vital to the reader's understanding of the lifecycle approach in the current version and how a strategically selected implemented ITIL approach can yield value to the U. S. public sector organization. With a history and foundation of basic ITIL concepts understood, previous research and case evidence regarding ITIL implementation within organizations will be presented to establish a baseline and to illustrate rationale as to why those implementation methods present implementation challenges for the U. S. government agency.

The ITIL processes that comprise the lifecycle will be discussed. The lifecycle is composed of Service Strategy, Service Design, Service Transition, Service Operation, Continual Service Improvement, and all related processes and functions.

Part of the implementation problem for the government organization is the lack of a skilled and ITIL trained workforce. It will be illustrated how an ITIL trained and skilled workforce can aid the organization's ITIL implementation. With continued federal budgetary constraints, it continues to be a challenge to find financial support for training initiatives within the government organization. It is often viewed that any limited financial surplus an organization has must be invested into current day to day operations to show a more immediate return.

Often when financial resources become scarce within a government organization, it is the employee training dollars that are the first to be reallocated to more operationally focused needs.

Due to the criticality of having an ITIL trained workforce to implement ITIL within the organization, this book will illustrate other cost saving methods to provide ITIL training to employees of a government agency. Government agencies are often composed of many different types of employees (Department of Defense civilians, military, contractors, and consultants) and this adds a unique training challenge that government organizations have that private organizations do not. This unique training challenge/constraint may be unique to the public organizational sector but need not prevent the U. S. government organization from providing the needed ITIL training to all of their employees regardless of employment type.

In line with employee training, ITIL certification will be discussed and explained. ITIL certification is the best and most recognized method to illustrate an organization's employee knowledge and understanding of ITIL and the level of that knowledge and understanding. The book will explain in detail the current ITIL certification scheme that takes employees from the basic foundation certification level to the highest level of ITIL certification; ITIL Expert (note: during the writing of this book, the ITIL Master Certification was in development).

The significant component of the work is the implementation strategy that is best suited for the U. S. government agency to employ in bringing ITIL into their business practices. Prior to an in depth discussion; the basics of an ITIL implementation will be addressed to include the two prevalent approaches: big bang and phased approaches. Research will show that the phased approach is best suited to most government agencies in their ITIL implementation because it reduces their risk exposure dramatically.

The major component of any U. S. government agency's implementation of ITIL is its full and complete understanding of their own agency's vision and objectives. It is vital that the agency understand "what they do that is important." This is the case because the agency's vision, objectives, and critical tasks will be tied to the ITIL process(s) that align most closely with their vision, objectives, and critical tasks. Additionally, this book will show that this implementation strategy will provide the agency with the greatest return on investment (ROI) for their ITIL implementation; a significant concern for any government entity. Based upon the two implementation approaches, the work will stress the value of the phased approach to the government agency as this will produce the greatest ROI as opposed to the big bang implementation approach.

Evidence will be gathered from a number of sources to support the implementation strategy presented here. Generic implementation data from other industries that is applicable to the government sector will be utilized. There is no "cookie cutter" ITIL implementation template that can be applied to every U. S. government agency. In other words, one agency may find that implementing a change management process is best and most cost effective first process to implement; whereas another agency may find that incident management is the best. Having a process to align an agency's vision, objectives, and employee critical tasks to the ITIL processes can provide to the agency which ITIL processes are best to implement and which may add little or no value. With agencies currently experiencing financial constraints and limitations; it is critical to have a process that allows agencies to "select" the ITIL process(s) that will benefit those most. This work will detail how this can be done.

Literature Review

Information Technology Infrastructure Library (ITIL) concept arose in the 1980's as a result of the British government determining that the level of IT service quality was not at an acceptable level (England, 2007). The Office of Government Commerce (OGC) was tasked with developing a framework that would address a more efficient and financially responsible method of managing IT services within the British government. For many years this initial framework was confined to the United Kingdom and other European communities. It was not until many organizations exhausted years of their IT budgets to prepare for Y2K that for most turned out to be a "non-issue" did the rest of the IT world realize that there must be a better way. It was during this timeframe that ITIL began to take a stronger foothold worldwide.

ITIL should not be considered a stagnant framework. In fact, it is currently the third version of the framework being completed in 2007 with a "refresh" in 2011. What started as a somewhat disjointed effort to define a community of practice for managing an organization's IT resources; evolved into more practical guidance with a universal appeal. Version 2 remains a popular option for organizations that embraced the concepts and lack the resources to move to Version 3. Significant differences exist in the two versions, but the overall concept behind ITIL remains.

Version 1 consisted of over 40 volumes of IT best practice that had limited practical use to the IT practitioner because of the vast amount of data contained in those 40+ volumes. It was quite a time consuming effort to locate the information applicable to a particular organization or business. Version 2 consolidated this effort and reduced the total volumes by nearly half with two primary volumes— Service Delivery and Service Support (Pollard & Cater-Steel, 2009). When Version 3 arrived in 2007, although most of the concepts and processes remained the same, the organization of the data changed. In Version 3, ITIL adopted a more service lifecycle approach. Therefore, the current version of ITIL contains only five volumes that encompass a lifecycle approach—Service Strategy, Service Design, Service Transition, Service Operation, and Continual Service Improvement.

With a framework in place, a critical part of the framework was absent (intentionally) that would make ITIL more practical for organizations and businesses of all shapes and sizes. Until recently, there has been little definitive research or guidance done to aid businesses and organizations in the methods used for bridging this framework into the day-to-day business activities. Where ITIL implementation is concerned, a literature search reveals that most implementation guidance's focuses on ITIL Value and implementation processes for private firms or foreign firms. Little or no research has been done that provides implementation guidance to United States public organizations or agencies; particularly at the federal level.

The vast majority of ITIL implementation research conducted today entails largely two distinct areas of emphasis. Both of these areas are research that is needed and provides value to the body of knowledge needed for all organizations to better understand what is involved in successfully implementing ITIL. Although, both of these areas have much merit, the argument is that neither goes far enough in a practical application sense to fully address the implementation questions based upon specific industry needs.

The first area of ITIL implementation research concerns the actual value of an ITIL implementation to the organization. Certainly this would be a good first step in evaluating whether the organization can expect real benefit from an implementation. If the results of this value research were to reveal a positive outcome; it would reveal little or no useful guidance on how to proceed further.

Perhaps an ITIL implementation may add value to the business or agency, but this research provides no guidance on the implementation approach or the methods needed to incorporate ITIL into current business practices. This is the area where this implementation research falls short. Knowing that an agency should start an ITIL implementation initiative and knowing where to start are separate and distinct issues.

Research on methods and procedures to actually incorporate ITIL within an organization has been done, but is limited at best. Much of this published guidance is generic in nature and fails to address specific organizational differences. Some research is evident on ITIL implementation within foreign governments; however little research exists that address the unique challenges that face United States government agencies. This is the gap in the existing research that this book will attempt to address with a recommended solution. The real value of an ITIL implementation will be discussed initially in this literature review.

Business Value of an ITIL Implementation

The first step in any ITIL implementation; government agency or otherwise, is to make an assessment as to whether there is value in doing so. A recent survey by Evergreen Systems revealed that 50.5% of the executives interviewed claimed that they did not approve ITIL implementations for their organizations because the business value of these implementations could not be proven (Evergreen Systems, 2006). The figure below illustrates the results of the survey with the top four barriers to an ITIL implementation highlighted. Resistance to change can likely be found in nearly any organizational change endeavor, and any organizational change requires leadership support to be successful. Lacking a clear vision as to where to start with an ITIL implementation is at the very heart of this question; but also suggests these organizations may lack the basic ITIL training and knowledge needed for such an effort. Options available to organizations to provide their employees the ITIL skills needed is also addressed in later sections of this paper.

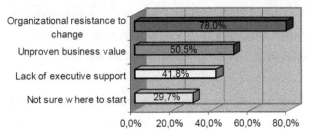

Figure 1 – Significant Barriers to ITIL Adoption/Implementation (Evergreen Systems, 2006)

There exist methods and procedures that can aid organizations in determining if an ITIL implementation would provide value to the business. Research has been done that can be of assistance in this "first step" endeavor. However, it is important to remember that this research alone will not get the organization to the ITIL Promised Land. But the existing research and knowledge that has been done is a valued starting point.

There is not much directly related academic research that provides Return on Investment (ROI) specifically for ITIL implementations (Tiong, Cater-Steel, & Tan, 2009), but adaptive techniques can be utilized from investment analysis methods that can be applied to an ITIL implementation in much the same manner as any organizational change implementation. Value analysis can be attempted for an ITIL implementation from a financial or management perspective. ROI, Net Present Value (NPV), Internal Rate of Return (IRR), and Payback Period (PBP) can be those financial analysis approaches and Benefits Management can be the management or investment approach.

Although little research has been done to apply any of these value analysis techniques to ITIL, a literature review does reveal some evidence of research in this area. Research conducted by Pedro Carmo Belo de Oliveira highlighted the importance of ROI, NPV, IRR, and PBP in illustrating that ITIL value to the organization can be illustrated using value analysis techniques. To aid the ITIL implementer, he went so far as to illustrate the advantages and disadvantages of each technique as illustrated in the table below (Oliveira, 2009).

Metrics	Advantages	Disadvantages
NPV	• Takes under consideration the discount rate.	• Does not give any indication about the project's magnitude and risk. • Discount rate can be hard to calculate.
ROI	• Perfect for one-to-one project comparison. • Commonly used. • Takes under consideration the cost of capital.	• Does not give any indication about the project's magnitude. • Requires vendors to share "sensible" information. • Can only compare project with the same level of risk. • Does not recognize when the cash flows take place.
IRR	• Identifies investments with irregular profits. • Takes under consideration the discount rate.	• Not easy to compute and understand. • Does not give any indication about the project's magnitude. • Assumes that the cash inflow from an investment is reinvested at the same discount rate. • Hurdle rate varies from company to company.
PBP	• Expresses the time it takes for an investment to reach the 'break even' point. • Separates, in terms of risk, long-term from short-term investments.	• Does not take under consideration the discount rate. • Does not give any indication about the project's magnitude. • No information about the investment performance after the 'breakeven' point. • Does not identify when the cash flows take
EVA	• CIOs analyze investment with shareholder's lens. • Easy to understand. • Simple methodology. • Calculation includes cost of capital charges.	• Cannot be used by organizations that are not publicly traded. • EVA is uncertain. • Cost of capital varies from organization to organization.

Table 2 – Comparison of Value Analysis Techniques (Oliveira, 2009).

The IT Service Management Academy published a White Paper that highlighted the value justification of an ITIL implementation using some of the value analysis techniques listed previously (Lewis & Schwartz, 2009). Cases were cited and broken out by industry type. A few examples are listed below:

- In 2002, VISA implemented ITIL Incident Management process resulting in incident resolution times being reduced by 75%.
- Using ITIL processes, the Ontario Justice Enterprise created a virtual help desk; reducing support costs by 40%.
- Purdue University trained 250 of their full time staff. Implemented an ITIL-based Service Desk and were able to cut second level support calls by 50%.
- After implementing ITIL, Multicare, a healthcare company, reduced a backlog of trouble tickets from 700 to 50 in only 6 months.
- As a result of ITIL implementation, Hershey Foods achieved a 97% success rate on infrastructure changes made. Only 3% of changes required roll back to the original state.
- As a result of implementing ITIL, the Auto Club Group experienced a decrease in service outages by 86%.

These example cases cited in the ITSM Academy White Paper illustrate value to the business that can be realized with a successful ITIL implementation. These organizations performed a value analysis of an ITIL implementation and determined there was business value in proceeding with an implementation.

As this section of the Literature Review suggests, Mr. de Oliveira and others have conducted research and provided some useful guidance and prior case study evidence regarding whether an organization should invest the needed resources to implement ITIL; but this fails to address the problem as to "how" to implement ITIL tailored to a specific industry. Although value assessment of an ITIL implementation fails to provide definitive implementation guidance, the literature review did reveal some general ITIL implementation guidance. This will be addressed in the following section.

Procedural Guidance to Implement ITIL

The literature review does reveal that some practical implementation guidance exists. Although limited in scope, Malcolm Fry and Sharon Taylor have provided their own brand of implementation guidance to businesses. Again, this guidance is not specifically focused on the U.S. government sector, or addresses the budgetary constraints that most government agencies are experiencing; but this research and guidance does warrant addressing in this literature review.

In Malcolm Fry's book "ITIL Lite: A Road Map to Full or Partial ITIL Implementation," he addresses a salient point as to why a partial implementation is not to be feared (Fry, 2010). This is a significant point being made by Mr. Fry and is particularly applicable to a government agency that would be forced to implement in parts versus the whole due to a lack of skilled ITIL practitioners or financial resources to accomplish a full implementation. Explaining "why" something should be done without the corresponding "how" it should be done creates a significant problem. It would be unfair to say that Mr. Fry does not provide the "how" to implementation. He does, but in a different manner that is needed for a government entity. He recommends categorizing all ITIL processes and functions into 4 distinct groups as a method to arrive at a LITE approach to implementation. This may arrive at an acceptable implementation approach for some businesses, but for the government agency, it would provide no greater assurance that once implemented the processes or functions was the correct financial choice for that agency. Although Mr. Fry's approach could be an effective method for some organizations, it lacks in its ability to guide the organization in implementing processes with the greatest return on investment first.

This is what is of particular importance for the government agency that is faced with budget constraints and fewer resources.

Sharon Taylor and Ivor Macfarlane wrote a book that provides insightful guidance on implementing ITIL; but addresses the implementation in a small scale environment (Taylor & Macfarlane, 2005). Small businesses can benefit from an ITIL implementation, so the benefits of this literature should not be ignored. But the direct applicability to a large U.S. government agency is lacking. This text fails to directly address the financial constraints of an implementation or a definitive method for process implementation in rank order based upon projected return on investment. This is the underlying need of the large U.S. Government agency that existing research has failed to adequately address.

The available literature seems to suggest that few acceptable methods of ITIL implementation exist that can ensure success. The underlying issue is that any "cookie-cutter" implementation approach cannot be successful for every industry type. The industry type must decide how best to utilize the processes of ITIL to benefit the industry and specific organization within that industry. The review was unable to discover any definitive implementation guidance specifically designed to aid a U. S. government agency in its ITIL implementation efforts. This is the issue/problem that this book will attempt to address. Results will provide the U. S. government agency with definitive guidance on how best to implement ITIL within the agency with the greatest potential return on their investment.

Methodology

The methodology used will be more qualitative than quantitative in design. The research will attempt to understand the distinctive differences in implementing ITIL within a U. S. government agency as opposed to private company counterparts. Prevailing research fails to provide definitive guidance for the government agency in their efforts to implement ITIL. Using a qualitative research method, the book will attempt to gather an in-depth understanding of the unique challenges experienced by government agencies in their implementation attempts and suggest possible solutions to those challenges; providing new ITIL implementation guidance to the U. S. government agency.

Discussion and Results

History of ITIL

One of the prevailing myths of ITIL is that there is no need to have an understanding of the history and origins of ITIL prior to undertaking efforts to implement it within an organization. This statement could not be further from the truth. To fully understand any subject and how to properly use it, it is imperative to have an understanding of its impetus and the reasons behind its existence and development. This is not possible without a basic understanding of the history of the subject. This section will briefly discuss the history of ITIL, why it was needed, and why it has stood the test of time in comparison to similar methodologies.

When technology departments began to be added to businesses and organizations in efforts to improve the customer's experience through technology, most of these businesses had little understanding for how these IT departments actually impacted the business and ultimately the customers. Most of the employees that made up these departments were skilled in the technical side of the department with little knowledge of management or understanding of the business they were supporting. Over time, managers began to become concerned with the overall efficiency of their IT infrastructures and its ability to support their customers. This concern led to a number of initiatives to improve IT efficiency which included brainstorming sessions, focus groups, and work simplification programs. Although bringing improved efficiencies to the IT department was a valued business goal, often these initiatives faded almost before they started.

It is not uncommon for an organization's newly appointed leader to institute some form of improvement initiative when appointed to their position. Often once this leader departs the organization, so does that initiative. Other times, initiatives are begun without the full support of organizational leadership or a primary supporter with enough influence to sustain the effort. Without this support, there is little opportunity for the initiative to take a foothold within the organization.

Business competition can often supply the spark for an initiative to take root. In the late 1980s a series of process management initiatives took hold in American industry. These initiatives focused on methods to improve the quality of products and services an organization offers to its customers. Continuous Process Improvement (CIP) and Total Quality Management (TQM) are two such efforts that took shape during this time. Only limited use of these (and others) is still in use today. The comings and goings of such initiatives suggests that these programs are easy to start, difficult to sustain, and usually have a short life cycle. What makes ITIL different from other similar initiatives?

Perhaps the most significant reason why ITIL has not only stood the test of time but has begun to flourish may be its linkage to service management. Whereas Service Management has emerged from so many varied points of view it has often been difficult to settle on an established definition that the world would fully embrace. In his book, "At America's Service," Karl Albrecht seemed to capture the basics of the concept when he stated, " Service management is a total organizational approach that makes quality of service, as perceived by the customer, the number one driving force for the operations of the business." (Albrecht, 1988). ITIL embraces this concept fully and then adds the organization's IT infrastructure to the discussion. Service management was not always at the forefront or prevalent in any way within many organization's IT departments. In the first decade or so of the IT revolution, there was little or no emphasis placed on IT service management or how the efforts of that business department impacted their customers. IT service management changed all that and led to the development of three primary objectives of IT service management: (Schiesser, 2010).

1. To ensure that the organization's business needs are supported by high-quality, cost-effective, value-adding IT services.
2. To improve the quality of IT service provision.
3. To reduce the long-term cost of IT service provision.

Now that the origins and sustainability of ITIL have been addressed, it is appropriate to provide some historical perspective on the evolution of ITIL. Not only will the following paragraphs describe how ITIL came into being and why, but also will describe its transformation from then to the present day.

It is commonly accepted that ITIL's history can be traced back to the middle 1980's in Great Britain. The British government realized that its vast bureaucracy had become more dependent on computers and technology to process large quantities of data necessary to support their citizens and customers. The British government also realized that the more dependent they became on these computer systems, the job they were doing in providing reliable services to their users dramatically declined. What had been put into place to streamline operations (computer systems) had ultimately created additional burdens and caused existing processes to become less efficient.

In 1986, the British government authorized the Centralized Telecommunications and Computing Agency (CTCA) to sponsor a program to promote improved efficiencies in the management of IT services (Petti, 2012). The agency issued a call to public, private, and academia sectors of the country to come forward with ideas and to establish a best practice framework for managing within the IT environment. The result of this effort was the publication of over 40 books in 1989 that became the first version of ITIL. This was a monumental effort to be sure; however to ask the ITIL practitioner to fully understand 40 books prior to being able to utilize the framework was less than realistic. It was clear from the outset that version one was only the beginning and that ITIL would need to undergo additional transformations prior to being a framework that the practitioner could fully embrace.

By the mid 1990's, the volumes that made up ITIL version one had swelled to 60 and had become extremely unwieldy. Based largely on input from an organization formed in the Netherlands called the Information Technology Service Management Forum (itSMF), work began to condense the 60 books to something more manageable. The end result of ITIL version 2 (V2) was a sizable reduction of the material from 60 books to only seven. The texts that comprised V2 were: Service Support; Service Delivery; Security Management; Application Management; Information & Communication Technology (ICT) Infrastructure Management; Planning to Implement Service Management; and The Business Perspective. This was a significant departure from version one in that the volume of material was vastly reduced. Furthermore, the bulk of the practical material was contained within only two books; Service Support and Service Delivery. In fact, these two books contained the bulk of the material on which ITIL certification was based (ITIL industry certification schema is discussed and explained later in the section).

In 2000, a number of ITIL related events occurred. In Great Britain, the CCTA merged into the Office of Government Commerce (OGC) therein cementing the idea that IT should serve the business and not the other way around (Rasa, Kumar, & Wahida Banu, 2010). Microsoft became one of the first American companies to embrace ITIL and the publication of the first of the V2 books (Service Support) were two other major ITIL events to start the new millennium. It was a relatively short period of time before it was realized that ITIL required another major revision.

Version 3 retained the IT focus on providing services to customers and users; however included the concept that services can best be explained and utilized within the context of a lifecycle. This change's most significant contribution was the introduction of services as a lifecycle. V3 describes the service as having five distinct stages throughout its life. They include Service Strategy, Service Design, Service Transition, Service Operation, and Continual Service Improvement.

ITIL was almost exclusively a European concept until the turn of the century when it began to make some traction in the United States. There have been many theories as to why the United States lagged behind the European community in its adoption of ITIL. Additionally, many scholars have speculated as to which triggers actually spawned its emergence into the United States early in the 21st century.

The global war on terrorism has often been listed as one impetus to the interest in ITIL within organizations in the United States. The threat of failed infrastructure was never greater in the minds of business leaders than after the 9/11 attacks. A single threaded data center, if wiped out, could require thousands of man-hours to restore and cost a considerable amount of money and business capital to bring the business back to a pre-attack status. Part of the ITIL V2 methodology details continuity planning strategies, of which was of particular importance to business leaders post 9/11.

A second trigger for the advancement in ITIL interest in the United States was the further globalization of the world economy. During this time, many American companies had decided to open up data centers and other business units in overseas locations. In doing so, many of these American company leaders saw the benefits of their European counterpart's use of ITIL processes and this sparked their interest. Much of what was observed was brought back and the news of ITIL success overseas began to spread within the American corporate environment. Certainly arguments suggesting other triggers impacted the initiation of ITIL in the

U. S. is just as valid, the two listed above are presented here only to illustrate the kind of event or situation that need be present to influence ITIL use in the United States.

The adage, "you must know where you have been before you can know where you are going" is a testament to the importance of understanding the history of a subject. This is as true for ITIL as it is for any other subject. It would be exceedingly difficult to proceed with this effort without a background understanding of where ITIL came from and how it has transformed into what it is today.

Concluding this section of this book, at a recent IT Service Management conference offered by the internationally known IT Service Management company, Pink Elephant, Rich Petti presented an introductory discussion on ITIL that included the following slide. The following slide presents some of the basic historical highlights of ITIL throughout the years. Listed in the Appendix of this paper for reference is a more detailed table with the historical highlights of ITIL.

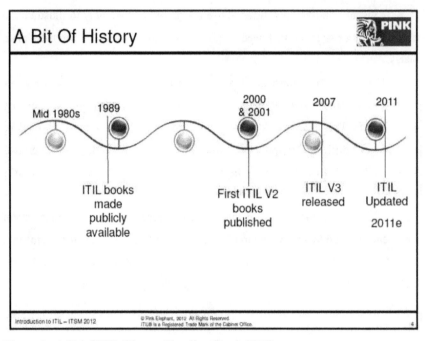

Figure 3: A Brief ITIL History Timeline (Petti, 2012).

ITIL Processes (Lifecycle)

As was mentioned in the previous section on ITIL history, the current version of ITIL (V3) has embraced a service lifecycle approach. Many ITIL training providers and consulting companies have made attempts to explain this lifecycle approach with a basic figure wheel. The example provided below by Syntel Inc, an ITIL training and consulting company, captures the interrelationships among the lifecycle phases and processes well.

Figure 4: ITIL Version 3 Service Lifecycle (Syntel, 2012).

At the core of the figure above is Service Strategy signifying the importance that strategy plays in supporting the other phases of ITIL V3. Service Design feeds into Service Transition and then into Service Operation. From there it repeats or continues again based upon input provided by output from the Continual Service Improvement phase; illustrated by the outer circle. Syntel thought to include some processes and their relationship to the applicable lifecycle phase which is a helpful addition to the traditional V3 lifecycle graphic. For example, Incident, Problem, and Event Management are illustrated with Service Operation which is the lifecycle phase in which these processes occur.

As with an understanding of the history of ITIL, without an understanding of the ITIL lifecycle phases and the corresponding processes, an ability to implement ITIL at any level within any business environment would be increasingly challenging or perhaps impossible. It is therefore prudent at this point to spend some time discussing the five lifecycle phases of ITIL and their most relevant processes. It should be noted that it is not practical nor within the scope of this book to address all aspects of the ITIL lifecycle and associated processes. Only those concepts most significant to a basic understanding of the phase or process; or implementation related, will be addressed. Service Strategy and its associated processes will be addressed first.

Service Strategy

As is suggested in the above figure, Service Strategy serves as the centerpiece of the ITIL lifecycle. Service Strategy delivers guidance in developing service management as a strategic resource for the business. This phase of the lifecycle helps the organization develop a usable ITIL strategy that can be incorporated into their business strategy. Strategy is often related to the military world where in this context the application and distribution of resources are utilized to accomplish a particular objective of a military plan or to defeat an adversary. It is not much different in the IT Service Management arena. The goal of Service Strategy is to identify the competition (adversary) and to compete with them by distinguishing oneself from the rest by delivering superior performances (van Bon, et al., A Management Guide: Service Strategy based on ITIL V3, 2008). IT Service Strategy addresses a number of key concepts that aid the organization in being able to do this. A large part of a Service Strategy is determining whether a service provides value to the business/organization or not. Customers value IT service when they see a distinct relationship between that IT service and the business value they need to produce. The level of value the customer perceives from the IT service is made up of two separate but related components: Utility and Warranty (Adams, 2009).

With regards to IT services, utility is fitness for purpose and warranty is fitness of use. The service customer or user's perception regarding utility is derived based on whether the service has a positive effect on the performance of tasks associated with a desired outcome. The removal or lessening of constraints on performance is also viewed positively by customers. Warranty happens when a service is available when needed, in enough capacity, dependable in regards to continuity, and secure. If a customer were evaluating a data storage service to determine if it created value to the business, utility would be evaluated in terms of data storage performance and any possible performance constraints. At least positive performance or lack of constraints results in the service being fit for purpose. It does not pass the value test until it passes the warranty test as well. If the proposed data storage service is available when needed, have the required capacity, dependability, and security it is deemed fit for use. So, as perceived by the customer, if the service is both fit for purpose and fit for use than it is deemed to be a value creating service. The figure below illustrates this concept graphically.

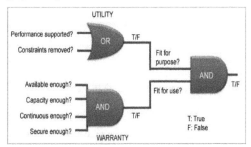

Figure 5: Logic of Service Value Creation (Bhatti, 2012).

IT service customers must have services fit for purpose and use. Service providers must offer services that create value for their customers. Purchasing value (by the customer) and producing and offering value (by the service provider) are cornerstone strategic outcomes for both parties and are a foundation of ITIL's Service Strategy. Within this lifecycle phase, there are three processes that will be discussed: Financial Management, Service Portfolio Management, and Demand Management.

Financial Management

Any service that provides value to a business or customer is going to have costs involved. This process aids both the customer and service provider in addressing those cost concerns. Financial Management provides the business and IT with the quantification, in financial terms, of the value of IT services, the value of the assets underlying the provisioning of those services, and the qualifications of operational forecasting (Iqbal & Nieves, 2007). ITIL's Financial Management process aids the business and service provider in assessing exactly what it will cost for the establishment of a particular IT service. For example, a United States government agency puts out a Request for Proposal (RFP) seeking solutions for an agency wide Faxing/Printing Service for their agency employees. They do this because they wish to deliver value to their employees by facilitating outcomes their employees what to achieve without the ownership of the direct costs and risks. Coincidently, the previous statement is very similar to the ITIL definition of a service.

A Faxing/Printing Service for an agency is not as simple as a service provider installing a number of high end printers and fax machines in the agency and developing some form of "chargeback" method to the agency for the service. Any RFP will likely have multiple responses from service providers attempting to secure the bid. All must strategically determine how to best deliver the service at a value that is required at a cost that will allow the provider to see a return significant enough to make the venture worthwhile. The government contracting world is full of instances where a service provider under bid for a contract, was awarded the work, only to find that ultimately they were losing money at an alarming rate and was forced to cut costs by either laying off employees or reducing the level of service that was originally requested in the RFP. This can happen for any number of reasons; for example, simple service provider greed, failure to fully understand the RFP requirement, or failure to follow ITIL's financial management methodology to properly assess the true value and cost of the service.

ITIL's Financial Management cautions both the service provider and business that there are numerous costs associated with providing a service that creates value. Some of these costs that must be taken into consideration are listed below:

1. Hardware and software license costs.
2. Annual maintenance fees for the hardware and software
3. Personnel resources used in the support or maintenance of the service
4. Utilities and other facility charges
5. Taxes, capital and interest charges
6. Compliance costs (governance)

ITIL's Financial Management is a strategic process that is critical in ensuring the service value is at a level that is acceptable to both service provider and customer. Additionally, Financial Management provides direct input into the next Service Strategy process-Service Portfolio Management.

Service Portfolio Management

The service portfolio is a method to describe a provider's available service in terms of value to the business. It describes the business' needs and the provider's responses to those needs. This process is a method for governing investment in service management across the enterprise while managing the available service's value. The most significant output from Service Portfolio Management (SPM) is the service portfolio itself.

The portfolio represents a service provider's investment and commitment to all customers and market spaces. It represents current contract commitments, efforts in developing new service offerings, and current ongoing efforts to improve existing services. Within the portfolio is the Service Catalog which is the visible part of the portfolio to the customers. The catalog lists all approved services that the service provider offers to potential customers. These services are those that are approved and currently in service operation status due to the due diligence performed regarding risks and costs of the services. Resources are fully available from the service provider to support all active services. Also within the catalog are the retired services. Although retired service are no longer actively offered to customers for purchase, they remain in the catalog so their transition out and contractual obligations to existing customers can be properly managed. Although the intent of retired services is to cease offering of these services to customers, under special circumstances between the service provider and customer it is possible to reactivate phased out services.

Another part of the portfolio is the Service Pipeline. These are the services of a provider that are "under construction." The pipeline of services represents the service provider's attempts at growth and strategy in looking toward future company growth. An example of a service in the pipeline may be a new and innovative type of IT service that the provider believe will be attractive to its customers and of course, provide added value to them.

Service Portfolio Management with the Service Portfolio (and accompanying service catalog and pipeline) is a critical process within the Service Strategy lifecycle. This process allows customers to visualize the service offerings of the provider along with the level of service provided; with customer costs for each service. The final process within the Service Strategy lifecycle is Demand Management.

Demand Management

Managing user demand for services is a critical Service Strategy process. Poorly managed or the inability to manage demand is a source of risk for all service providers. At its very heart, Demand Management is activities that understand and influence customer demand for services and the provision of capacity to meet these demands. At a strategic level Demand Management can involve analysis of patterns of business activity and user profiles. At a tactical level it can involve use of differential charging to encourage customers to use IT services at less busy times (Iqbal & Nieves, 2007) at reduced costs to the customers.

The ability to manage service demand is critical at both ends of the spectrum. Customers are reluctant to pay for something that they are unable to use to its full capacity. Insufficient capacity has impact on the quality of services delivered and limits the growth of that service. This service demand incompatibility can be financially damaging to both the service provider and the service user.

For example, a service provider provides a certain amount of network bandwidth for a government agency to use. This bandwidth is available 24/7.

However, for the agency the bandwidth is only used to its fullest during the day when the majority of the agency's workers are on the job. At night the bandwidth, while still available, goes virtually unused. Understandably, a customer is unwilling to pay full price for a service that is only used at half its full value. A service provider needs maximum use of its provided services to produce maximum revenue. Being able to manage this problem is at the core of ITIL's Demand Management.

There are a number of ways the bandwidth demand example listed above could be managed. The service provider could offer discounted pricing to the agency if they utilized more bandwidth at night and less during the day. Another option to the service provider would be to offer the available night bandwidth to another agency (perhaps one in an overseas location during their peak usage times) when their demand is highest.

The principles of Demand Management help the service provider attain the greatest return on their investment for the IT services provided while ensuring the customer receives real value for the services they are using. ITIL's Service Strategy and its associated processes provide a framework for creating service value that both provider and customer will find attractive. With a strategy in place, Service Design phase of the lifecycle is necessary to create the services that will be put into operation by the customers utilizing these IT services.

Service Design

In keeping with ITIL's lifecycle approach to managing IT services; once the strategy has been fully addressed, it now comes time to design these services. This phase is concerned with developing appropriate IT services that meet the needs of current and future customers. Included within this design phase would be the architecture, processes, policy, and documentation of these services. The actual design goal is to meet the current and future business requirements of the prospective customers of these services.

In order for these newly developed (or modified) services to meet all customer expectations and requirements the following must be considered during the design phase of the lifecycle (van Bon, et al., A Management Guide: Service Design based on ITIL V3, 2008):

--Any new service must be added to the service portfolio and must be kept up to date as the service changes.

--The Service Level Requirements (SLR) must be clearly defined before the service is delivered to the customers.

--Based on the SLR, the capacity management team can model the new requirements based on the current infrastructure.

--If it appears that a new or improved infrastructure or resources are needed to support the new service, financial management must be involved.

--A Business Impact Analysis (BIA) should be performed to assess if the new service poses any risks. If so, this will provide valuable information to IT Service Continuity Management (ITSCM).

--The Service Desk must be educated on the new service and how to respond to customer inquiries regarding that service.

--Service Transition can assist in bringing this new service into the operational environment.

--Supplier Management must be involved if there are parts or equipment needed for the new service.

It should be noted that many of this lifecycle phase's processes are either directly or indirectly mentioned in the list above. Each of these will be discussed briefly later in this section.

The Service Design phase of the ITIL lifecycle begins when a request for a new or modified service is received by the IT provider from a customer. Ultimately, at the end of the design phase, a service solution must be presented that meets all the requirements of the customer. This design solution could be anything from a simple software program that provides a new or modified functionality for a small group of users to a new building complete with a massive IT infrastructure capable of supporting hundreds of employees. Regardless of the design scope, the end result is the same. The design solution should deliver exactly what is specified in the customer requirement—no more functionality than was requested and no less.

A design that exceeds the customer's requirements risks delivering a service that does not meet the needs of the customer at an increased cost to the service provider. A design that falls short on delivering what the customer requested causes rework at the expense of the service provider and delays in the deliverable to the customer. This can also result in a less favorable opinion of the service provider by the customer that could result in future lost business opportunities for the provider. It is clear that the service design should match the customer requirement exactly; as this produces the greatest benefit to both parties.

There are a number of ITIL processes that fall within Service Design and these will be briefly addressed next in this section of this book. Service Level Management will be discussed first.

Service Level Management

The Service Level Management (SLM) process of ITIL is much like the mediator between the business and the service provider. It helps to ensure that the design that was agreed to is actually met when the design is delivered to the customer. SLM process may have its beginnings in the Design phase of the ITIL lifecycle but it transgresses across many of the other phases of the lifecycle as well. This is evident in the official SLM definition which states that SLM negotiates, agrees, and documents appropriate IT service targets with representatives of the business, and then monitors and produces reports on the service provider's ability to deliver the agreed levels of service (Lloyd & Rudd, 2007). This SLM definition strongly suggests that this process extends through all aspects of the ITIL lifecycle. It is easy to see that SLM exists in the Service Operation phase (monitoring of the levels of service) and the Continual Service Improvement phase (if targets are not met, re-negotiation of the acceptable levels must take place during CSI). Due to the criticality of the customer and service provider agreeing on the level of performance the service will provide, this initial agreement must be reached prior to the final design of that service. This is why the most appropriate lifecycle phase of SLM is the ITIL Service Design phase. Axios Systems, a leading ITIL IT Service Management solutions provider, has illustrated this customer/service provider connection brought about by the SLM process in the figure below:

Figure 6: SLM: The Bridge to Client/Service Provider Agreement (ITIL Service Level Management Software, 2012).

The figure illustrates how the business plan and requirements are passed to the service provider to develop a service design that meets those business requirements. In turn, the service provider would pass the final design package that meets their requirements back to the client customer for concurrence and approval. This customer/service provider exchange is held together by ITIL's SLM process. Part of any design of a service must include consideration for its availability to the customer base it is designed to serve. Availability Management aids in this endeavor.

Availability Management

Service Availability (and capacity for that matter) must be designed into the service from the very outset. The principle goal of Availability Management is to ensure that the level of service availability delivered matches or exceeds the current and future needs of the business, at an acceptable cost. This must be part of the agreement that was reached in the SLM process that was previously discussed. The SLM process goes much deeper than simply requesting e-mail service for an agreed price from the provider. The level of the service must be discussed and agreed too; and this is where other processes become significant.

What point would there be to a customer purchasing a service if there was no guarantee that the service was available when it was needed by the users? Clearly, a service with substandard availability does not benefit anyone; particularly the users of that service. The availability and reliability of IT services have a direct influence on customer satisfaction and the reputation of the service provider. So, both parties have a stake in making the service as reliable and available as cost effectively as possible.

There are a number of ways an organization and its service provider can agree on availability of a particular service and the granularity of that service's availability. For example, an organization may want to include availability metrics on the components that make up a particular service. The agreement may be that an e-mail server that supports the e-mail service must be reliable 99.9% of the time. There are a number of complicated methods to calculate service/component availability, but a rather simple method for illustration is the following:

Agreed Service Time – Downtime = Availability

Agreed Service Time (AST) is the time that the service or service component should be available for use based upon the agreement reached by the customer and provider. The AST could be stated that the availability will be 24 hours a day 7 days a week; or 10 hours / day between the hours of 10 AM to 8 PM, or any number of other specified methods. The key is that the AST must specify the service availability expectations. Downtime is the time when the service or service component was not available. An important note regarding downtime is that it is only considered when it happens during the AST (Lloyd & Rudd, 2007). A service outage that happens outside of the AST does not count against the service's availability report.

So, if a service was agreed to be available for 1000 hours during the span of a month, and during those 1000 hours, there were 50 hours of downtime; the service availability for that month would only have been 95%. Another concept that relates significantly to availability of a service is the capacity of that service. Capacity Management is also addressed in the Service Design phase of the lifecycle.

Capacity Management

Capacity deals with how much of a service a customer(s) needs now and in the future. Service Level Agreements (SLA) is often the driver for determining capacity requirements for a service. Both parties to the agreement must understand that unused capacity of a service results in a cost and insufficient use of a service also results in costs.

As an example, if an organization purchased a 512K network connection from a service provider so their users could have a connection to the internet and other network resource (the service); if over time only a small percentage of users actually used this connection at an average level of 128K used per month, this would be a misappropriation of the service capacity. The organization would be paying the service provider for a service (512K network connection) that is not being fully utilized; when a more cost effective 128K network connection may have been more appropriate for the organization.

On the other side, if the customer purchased a 128K connection and in reality there was a need for a much larger capacity connection due to an increased level of users; many users would be unable to connect to the network and would experience high levels of dissatisfaction with the service provider and perhaps the organization as well.

To say that Capacity Management is a delicate balancing act between the purchase price of the capacity of a service and the projected levels of that service's use is not an understatement. Capacity Management is initially supported in Service Strategy where decisions regarding the requirements of the business are made, customer outcomes of the service are projected, and the patterns of business activity (PBA) are evaluated. This provides the predictive and continuous capacity indicators that are needed to align the capacity of a service to the demand of the organization's users. The next process that must be addressed during the design phase of the ITIL lifecycle is that of IT Service Continuity Management.

IT Service Continuity Management

The goal of IT Service Continuity Management is to support the overall business continuity process by ensuring that the required IT technical and service facilities can be resumed within required and agreed business timescales (van Bon, et al., A Management Guide: Service Design based on ITIL V3, 2008). Quite often continuity management is something that an organization (public and private) get serious about only after the organization has experienced a disaster that has impacted its infrastructure, user's ability to access needed resources, and cost the organization staggering levels of financial resources to remedy. Organizations tend to either forget that these things do occur, or they simply hope that nothing bad will ever happen. Clearly, disasters do occur that can potentially cost a business more to rectify without any prior planning in place than had there been a recovery plan for the organization.

In what many consider the most significant work of business continuity management, Andrew Hiles' book, "The Definitive Handbook of Business Continuity Management," sites numerous cases of disasters that impacted businesses to an alarming level. He states the following statistics within his text: The World Disaster Report's 2009 Disaster Report announced that disaster deaths totaled 242,662. Of the 245 disasters in 2009, 224 were weather related impacting in some manner 55 million people; with an economic impact in excess of US$15 billion.   Within Mr. Hiles' book he further states that a recent study by ITIC/Stratus Technologies said that, although organizations know they need more reliable information systems, 49% have no budget for high-availability technology, 40% do not understand what qualifies as high availability and more than 80% cannot make the business case for it because they do not know the cost of downtime (Hiles, 2010). These are alarming figures from any business standpoint.

It can be a challenge to determine how to invest the often limited resources to ensure IT services are uninterrupted by disasters and other unforeseen events? Often a Business Impact Analysis and Risk Analysis can be a good starting point to determine which disaster events/service losses have the greatest impact to the business and must be addressed by an IT Service Continuity Strategy. The below figure illustrates a method to visually represent this process.

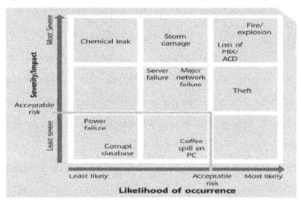

Figure 7: Example of summary risk profile (Lloyd & Rudd, 2007).

The figure above illustrates an organization's attempt to categorize events and service losses and their impact on the business. Any event/loss that falls within the acceptable risk level and is minimally severe to the business likely would not require any contingency management investment. However, those that are on the chart further up and to the right (like a major network outage or loss of phone service) are critical enough to the business to be included in an IT Service Contingency Plan.

The loss of critical IT infrastructure and services can have a crippling impact on organizations and ITIL's IT Service Continuity Management can provide the guidance needed to make critical decisions on how to best utilize the often limited contingency planning and implementation funds.

Service Catalog Management

This process is the development and upkeep of a service catalog that contains all the accurate details, the status, possible interactions and mutual dependencies of the current services available for purchase; and those services that are being proposed to be operational in the future. The service catalog was addressed in some detail within the Service Strategy lifecycle phase; specifically within the Service Portfolio Management phase. The actual management of the catalog itself is a critical component of ITIL and deserves its own processes within the Design phase for one very significant reason.

Over the years, the IT infrastructures of organizations have grown rapidly and there may not be a clear picture of all the services offered and to whom these services are offered to (not all users may be eligible to receive all services offered by a service provider) (van Bon, et al., A Management Guide: Service Design based on ITIL V3, 2008). Having a process in place to manage these service offerings is critical. The Service Design phase of the lifecycle is the logical phase for this process because as new service offerings are designed and placed into service, they can be added to the service catalog. Although the Service Portfolio and Catalog are related, a clear distinction can be drawn that justifies the need for two distinct ITIL processes.

Recall from the Service Strategy section that the portfolio contains information about each service and its status (active or inactive). As a result, the portfolio is a depiction of the entire service offering process starting with the customer requirement to the actual development and implementing of the specific service. The catalog, on the other hand, is a subset of the portfolio and consists only of the active and approved services that are in operation and available for use. This is what is visible to the clients/customers. For example, the catalog of IT services is much like a department store catalog that is advertised to its customers.

Details include items for sale, costs, specifications, and other specifics regarding the items (IT Services) for purchase by the department store's prospective customers. The principle is essentially the same for the IT service catalog developed and maintained by the IT service provider. Within the service portfolio, those services available to the customers exist, of course. However, other services are included as well that may not be customer facing as is the case with the catalog. Retired services and those still being developed by the service provider are all part of the service provider's portfolio of IT services.

With any IT service, providers and businesses alike must be concerned with the security of those services. ITIL V3's Information Security Management process is the next process within the Service Design phase of the lifecycle to be discussed.

Information Security Management

All aspects of an IT service's security must be designed into the service's development. This is the underlying reason why Information Security Management (ISM) process falls within the Service Design phase of the ITIL lifecycle. The goal of ISM is to ensure that IT security is also aligned with the policies of business security and is properly managed for all IT services and management activities and efforts.

Regarding any IT service, ISM's singular focus involves the four objectives of availability, confidentiality, integrity, and authenticity (van Bon, et al., A Management Guide: Service Design based on ITIL V3, 2008). These objectives will align with the same business security policies that the organization's leadership has put into place. Availability objective simply states that the information that is available from a particular service is present and useable when required. The confidentiality objective states that the information provided by the service is available exclusively to authorized individuals. Integrity objective deals with the information specifically. It states that the information is complete, accurate, and protected from any unauthorized changes. Authenticity refers to information interchanges between parties can be trusted as accurate representations of what was intended by the transaction.

With increased reliance on IT services comes the responsibility to secure those services. Businesses and other organizations that rely on these IT services must take steps to ensure adequate protective measures are in place. While legislatures have enacted governance measures that directly impact the corporate IT culture, many businesses seek additional assurances that their vendors and partners are taking the necessary steps to guard against security threats. The value of ISM cannot be overstated. ISM ensures that the Information Security Policy is maintained and enforced that fulfils the needs of the Business Security Policy and the requirements specified under the corporate governance directives. ISM manages all aspects of the IT and information security within all areas of IT services for an organization and the service provider.

ISM process within ITIL assists with ensuring all aspects of security are addressed with each IT service. Failure to adequately assess security with all newly developed IT services can cause these new services to be less effective than originally designed and planned. Without the ISM process in place, security incidents and risks could potentially jeopardize the likelihood of any designed IT service; thereby reducing the possibility that the IT service would be utilized by the customer. Any customer of a provided IT service needs assurance that the four objectives listed above are achieved by the efforts and tenants of the ITIL ISM process. Without this assurance, that particular IT service would be of little use to any customer concerned with IT security.

Supplier Management

Organizations must be in a position to clearly define their position with their suppliers and partners. ITIL's Supplier Management aids in being able to do this effectively. The goal of supplier management is to be able to manage suppliers and the services they supply, thereby providing seamless entry of their products or services into the process of providing quality services to the business. Suppliers and partners are an often forgotten and misunderstood contributor to the success or failure of the IT services that are used by the business. Supplier Management process assists the primary IT provider and the business with managing all party's expectations of the contributions to the service made by suppliers and partners. Supplier's entrance, contribution, and exit from the IT service chain can be illustrated by the below figure.

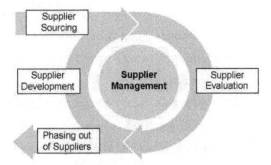

Figure 8:   Supplier/Partner Service contribution lifecycle (ITSM toolkits & templates & eLearning, 2012).

Suppliers enter and begin the contribution to an IT service by means of sourcing. Often an IT service provider will need to seek suppliers to provide network equipment to provide the IT service. Sourcing could entail soliciting bids from suppliers to deliver the needed equipment. Once a supplier is selected, they are evaluated to ensure the equipment being supplied continues to meet the needs of the IT service and the needs of the business. It continues to be the responsibility of the business and the IT provider to develop the supplier's expectations of the business' needs. As the business needs change, so to may the needs from the supplier change.

When the needs of the business no longer require the services provided by the supplier, they are phased out. For example, a supplier that makes Ethernet cables that was supplying this to an IT provider of Install services. If the organization changed to convert their infrastructure to Fiber, the Ethernet supplier would no longer be needed and would be phased out (assuming the supplier did not also manufacture Fiber cable). At this point, sourcing for a supplier of Fiber cable would be required to meet the needs of the business requirement.

Since most IT providers are unable to meet all the IT service needs and requirements of the business, contracts and agreements with suppliers and partners are critical for the success of the services provided to the businesses. Supplier Management process of the Service Design phase of the ITIL lifecycle is the key to ensuring supplier involvement is managed properly.

The preceding processes are all aimed at providing a focused approach to the design of IT services by service providers in response to customer requirements. With a strategy and service design in place, the ITIL lifecycle now turns to placing the service into the operational environment with the aid of ITIL's Service Transition lifecycle phase.

Service Transition

With the strategy and design of a service addressed, it is now time to put the newly developed service into operation. But a service cannot be placed into the operational environment of a business immediately after being developed. It must be transitioned into the operational environment. Why? For the answer to this question all that is needed to arrive at an answer is to ask virtually any IT operations individual. IT history is filled with incidents of service developers and designers deploying a new service without regards to a transitional period. The end result of this "tossing a new service over the fence to operations" is filled with potential dangers. Some of these dangers might be:

--implementing a new IT service that is replacing an older service which has not been properly decommissioned.

--Service Desk personnel are untrained on how to respond to user inquiries on the new service.

-- Users are untrained on how to utilize the new service.

--What impact does the new service have on existing services?

These are just a small sample of some of the potential problems and issues that may emerge if a new or modified service is placed into operation without being properly transitioned into the live business environment. Service Transition phase of the ITIL V3 lifecycle attempts to provide some structure in moving this service into the operational arena of the business; thereby minimizing potential problems when doing so.

This can be accomplished by ensuring that the service meets the requirements of the service specifications, by supporting the existing change process (if there is one) of the business, and by reducing variations in the performance and known errors of the new/changed services. These are all goals of Service Transition and highlight its role in the ITIL V3 lifecycle. Prior to addressing this lifecycle phase and its processes further, it is important to understand the phase's value to the business.

An effective Service Transition ensures that the new or changed services are being aligned with the customer's business operations. This is the true value to the business. Specifically regarding the following (van Bon, et al., A Management Guide: Service Transition based on ITIL V3, 2008):

--the capacity of the business to react quickly and adequately to changes in the market.

--changes in the business as a result of takeovers, contracting, etc. are well managed.

--more successful changes and releases for the businesses.

--better compliance of business and governing rules.

--less deviation between planned budgets and the actual costs.

--better insight into the possible risks during and after the input of a service.

--higher productivity of customer staff.

To that end, within ITIL's Service Transition phase, the Change Management, Service Asset & Configuration Management, Release & Deployment Management, and Knowledge Management processes can be utilized to reduce the likelihood the business will experience any adverse impact to the deployment or modification to a service. Perhaps the most significant and potentially impactful to the business is change. All businesses that rely on IT services are faced with making some form of change to their IT infrastructure at some point. Understanding the impact these changes may have to the customers and end users is critical. The example to lead off the Change Management section will clearly highlight this.

Change Management

Organizations that do not have a defined change management process in place run the risk of allowing IT technicians and engineers the ability to make changes to the network infrastructure without fully understanding the potential impact the work will have on users and other networking devices. For example, a few years ago, a router engineer at a U. S. government agency was making some "routine" access control list updates in a site's router and inadvertently isolated an entire site/node from all network resources; impacting thousands of users of these critical and mission essential resources. This event occurred prior to this agency establishing a change management process. At the time, network engineers were free to make network updates on networking equipment as was needed. As technically competent as most network engineers may be, it is difficult to fully assess the impact on the network as a whole (and its users) any single change may have without an approved change management process. This agency soon realized that developing a change management process across the agency enterprise would need to be a priority to prevent future "self-inflicted" network outages.

A change can be defined in many ways by many people. The addition, modification or removal of authorized, planned or supported service or service components and its associated documentation is the ITIL definition of a change (Lacy & MacFarlane, 2007). There are two basic types of changes; standard or routine and emergency changes. Routine changes are those that an organization has determined pose little risk and have been pre-authorized. In other words, the organization has already assessed these types of changes and has provided guidance on how to implement. Examples could include routine router maintenance actions that will not impact the operational environment, Upgrade of a user's PC, or perhaps an end-user's password reset may all be viewed as a routine change action. An emergency change is one that normally is intended to repair a failure on the network and has a large negative impact on the business.

Regardless of the type of change that is needed, it is critical that the Change Advisory Board (CAB) be involved in the change process for the organization. The change advisory board (CAB) is responsible for assessing the impact of requested changes and estimating the resource requirements. They will advise the change manager on whether changes should be approved and will assist in scheduling changes. CAB membership will depend on the change being requested and could consist of anyone who is potentially impacted by the change (Reboucas, Sauve, Maura, & Bartolini, 2007). The CAB will meet periodically to determine the impact of all Request for Changes (RFC) that have been submitted for evaluation. The CAB may approve or disapprove a RFC; or may go back to the requesting authority for more information regarding the change prior to making a decision. The CAB will often handle requests for non-critical types of changes. When there is an emergency situation, there may not be sufficient time to convene the entire CAB members to make a decision. In this case, an Emergency CAB will be convened which will include only a smaller contingent of organizational experts that can make emergency decisions regarding changes. Regardless, every single change must obtain approval prior to proceeding.

Although all organizations are free to develop their own activities and steps to deal with changes, the following is a commonly accepted practice.

--Create and Record the Change—A change is raised by a request from an initiator and properly documented. This is someone (or a group within the organization) that recognizes that a change is needed.

--Review the RFC - Stakeholders will verify if the RFC is actually warranted or if there are any problems with the RFC submission.

--<u>Assess and Evaluate Changes</u>—If the change is approved to go forward from the initial review, here is where the change impact must be evaluated. The 7 R's of Change management is a good starting point for change impact analysis as depicted below (Lacy & MacFarlane, 2007):

- Who raised the change?
- What is the reason for the change?
- What is the return required for the change?
- What are the change's risks?
- What resources does it require?
- Who are responsible for build, testing, and implementation?
- Which relationships exist between this and other changes?

--Formal authorization of the change – every change must be formally approved by the person or group that has the authority to grant such approval.

--Coordinate change implementation – Once authorized, the RFC should be passed to the relevant technical group that will perform the work; that is, build, test, and actually implement the change.

--Review and close out change record – did the change accomplish what it was intended to do? Were there any side effects to its implementation? This activity is used to review the change to make sure it accomplished what was intended. Included in the Appendix of this work is a figure that shows these change activities in a graphical manner.

Although there are other processes within Service Transition, change management is the cornerstone process within this phase of the ITIL V3 lifecycle. Service Asset and Configuration Management is the next process that will be discussed.

Service Asset & Configuration Management

All IT infrastructures have equipment that is placed throughout the organization that runs the IT network. Without these servers, routers, switches, computers, etc., IT services for the organization would be impossible. Service Asset & Configuration Management (SA & CM) is the process that ensures that all Configuration Items (CI) that make up an IT service are accounted for. SA & CM ensures that all components that form part of the service or product are identified, baselined, and maintained.

A service can only be as successful as the components that make up that service. If a large organization has an E-mail service that includes 20 e-mail exchange servers located throughout the organization, it is clear that the location of these servers, maintenance of the servers, software update schedules, and license agreement information, etc., be managed in some manner to keep the service they support from being interrupted. SA & CM process can aid in this success. The Configuration Management Database (CMDB) is a significant component of SA & CM. This database provides the definitive record of all CI's that make up the components of all IT services for the organization. There should be only ONE CMDB that is actively in use. There is an old adage that if you have one clock in your house, you always know what time it is. If you have more than one clock in your house, you can never really be certain what the real time is. This is as true for multiple CMDB's. If an organization has more than one CMDB's, if the info contained in both is not 100% identical, how would anyone know which CMDB is the most up to date and accurate? Clearly no one would ever be certain which one was the updated one. This is why there should only be one definitive CMDB.

A CMDB should include a rather exhaustive list of information regarding each and every CI that supports an organization's IT services. Often many organizations that have established a CMDB to document all the supporting CIs for their IT services will determine what information on each CI is needed to be maintained.   Some of the detailed information on each CI may include the following: A unique identifier, CI type, Name and description of the item, version, location of the item, license information, owner/custodian and contact information, status of item, historical data, and information and location of any applicable Service Level Agreements related to the CI.

It is critical to being able to manage the assets and configuration items that make up the IT services that are being provided to the business. If an IT provider is unable to locate the components/equipment that make up a business' IT service; when the service fails, it would significantly delay service restoration times while technicians attempted to locate and isolate the faulty component.   A fully functional Service Asset & Configuration Management process; particularly a well maintained CMDB can aid an organization in knowing where equipment is located within the organization, the service it supports, and who within the organization maintains the equipment when it becomes non-functional.

Release and Deployment Management

One aspect that changed during the "refresh" to V3 was that Release Management became Release and Deployment Management. This official name change for this process provides a suggestion as to the change in emphasis for this process to include the "deployment" of releases as just as significant an aspect to the process as the release itself. The importance of the roll out of the new or changed services into the live environment became of paramount concern (Klosterboer, 2009).

This process aims to build, test, and deploy the capability to provide the services specified by the Service Design and that will accomplish the stakeholders' requirements specified in Service Strategy. It is important to understand a few key release and deployment concepts when discussing deployment or release strategies—big bang vs. phased; Push and Pull; and Automation and Manual.

With the Big Bang deployment option is where a deployment of a new or changed service is sent out to all users in one operation. This option is often used when consistency of the service is critical across all users of the service. Of course the risk is that if something were to go wrong, the impact would be across all users and depending on the type of service being deployed, it could be catastrophic. In the phased approach, the service is deployed to a segment of the overall user base. This is often referred to as a pilot deployment. Remaining users receive the deployment by means of a scheduled rollout of the service. This option is often used when there are risks involved in the deployment and it has been determined that it is better to potentially only impact a smaller segment of the user base at a time; providing the opportunities to make deployment adjustments along the way, as necessary.

The difference between a push and pull release deployment is in the manner in which users received the release deployment. In a Push deployment, the new or improved service component is deployed from a center location out to the users. In a Pull deployment, the improved service component is made available in a central location and users are free to pull the update from that location at their convenience.

With today's technological advancements, the means of release deployment can be either automated or manual. Automation is often the preferred method because it ensures an amount of consistency in the deployment across the entire enterprise of users receiving the release. If manual means is used, it may be the preferred method if the release is of a small scale and can be monitored to ensure that potential errors are caught and corrected.

Regardless of how an organization attempts to deploy software releases, another process in the Service Transition lifecycle helps to ensure these releases are properly documented and storage of this vital data is managed and controlled in a consistent way throughout the organization. This process is known as Knowledge Management.

Knowledge Management

ITIL may include Knowledge Management (KM), but ITIL cannot take credit for the development of KM as a process. In fact, KM has been in existence in some form for thousands of years. Beginning 15,000 years ago competitive advantage was writing down the selected knowledge of merchants, artisans, physicians, and government administrators for future reference. Writing was used to create an enduring record of a society's rules, regulations, and cumulative knowledge. In Mesopotamia about 5,000 years ago, people began to lose track of the thousands of baked-clay tablets used to record legal contracts, tax assessments, sales, and law. The solution was the start of the first institution dedicated to Knowledge Management, the library (Bergeron, 2003). Although there are more advanced organizational knowledge capture methods and tools in use today, the underlying reasons for retaining corporate knowledge has changed very little over time.

Knowledge Management is often displayed in the Data to Information to Knowledge to Wisdom structure. Data is a set of discreet facts about events; information comes from providing a context to the data. Knowledge is composed of the tacit experiences, ideas, insights, and judgments of individuals. Wisdom gives the ultimate discernment of the material. The figure below provides a graphical representation of the relationships between data, information, knowledge, and wisdom and how each builds to a greater connectedness and understanding.

Figure 9: DIKW Model (Bellinger, Castro, & Mills, 2012)

Knowledge Management's intent is that the right information is available at the right time to the right person when needed. Organizational knowledge is critical for the success of any entity. How many times have we heard, "We cannot get that information or answer today, we must ask Joe when he returns to work tomorrow." Organizational knowledge and wisdom should not be stored in any one employee's head, but should be readily available to whoever in the agency has a justifiable need to know. The one big concern of any manager should be that if one employee has particular knowledge vital to that organization and departs for other employment (perhaps with a competitor) what happens to that knowledge?

ITIL V3 provides a KM solution aimed to the IT Services that a provider supplies. The Service Knowledge Management System (SKMS) is a set of tools and databases that are used to manage knowledge and information. The SKMS includes the Configuration Management System as well as other tools and databases. The SKMS stores, manages, updates, and presents all information that an IT Service Provider needs to manage the full lifecycle of IT Services (Lacy & MacFarlane, 2007).

Keeping knowledge controlled yet accessible to those with a need to know is often the challenge for any KM process; but there are a number of software tools that can aid the organization in accomplishing this challenging task. In the past, often a system administrator could set up a "share drive" on an organization's network that would allow a group to have access to the data and knowledge stored there. This soon became a bit unwieldy for large organizations as many share drives were needed with varying levels of access. Realizing a need, many software vendors have created various knowledge sharing and storage solutions to meet the KM needs of customers worldwide. One well used solution is that of Microsoft SharePoint. This allows the convenience of one URL link to access (and remember), but with the advantage of limiting access to components of the SharePoint site. Remember that not everyone in the organization should have the same level of access to all data stored on the SKMS. For example, perhaps everyone does not need to know what the Service Provider charges customers for each service; so perhaps financial data is restricted to the organization's financial department. MS SharePoint allows an administrator to allow, yet restrict access to the stored knowledge. There are obviously other software providers that produce similar products. It is the organization's duty to select that product that best suits their KM needs; now and into the future.

Service Transition and its associated processes are all aimed at smoothly moving newly created or modified IT services into the operational environment of the organization. This is where the organizational benefits of these services are realized by the business. The next ITIL V3 lifecycle phase-Service Operation-is where these services are put into practice for the organization. Service Operation is the next phase to be discussed in the next section.

Service Operation

With Service Strategy, Design, and Transition phases of the ITIL V3 lifecycle addressed along with their associated processes, it is now time to discuss the phase "where the rubber meets the road." Service Operation is where the services are actually put into practice for the customer. The benefits that the customers envisioned when the service was purchased are realized (hopefully). Service Operation (SO) is the point in the ITIL lifecycle where the delivery of the service to the customer takes place by the act of a service provider performing a set of procedures and/or activities. SO is more than just the repetitive execution of a standard set of procedures or activities. All functions, processes and activities are designed to deliver a specified and agreed level of service, but they have to be delivered in an ever-changing environment (Cannon & Wheeldon, 2007). This is one of the more challenging aspects of SO; as the business and technology environments change over time, services must continue to be delivered to the business at the agreed levels of service at an acceptable cost.

Service Operation is consistently challenged to balance the quality of the services delivered versus the costs of those services. For all services being provided, there is an agreed level of services that is promised. The challenge is to maintain this level at an optimum cost and resource utilization level. Although this may seem to be a straightforward premise, in the current global economic times, organizations are under severe pressure to increase the quality of service while reducing costs. This may seem like a contradiction in terms; how can quality increase while reducing costs? However, it is possible to increase service quality while reducing costs. Initiation for this goal usually occurs in Service Operation while fully formalized in the Continual Service Improvement phase of the ITIL lifecycle. Some cost savings initiatives can be done incrementally over time whereas other measures are savings that are realized only once. For example, if there are two similar software tools that do essentially the same thing for the customer; the reduction of one tool will be a one-time cost savings. Additionally, if a service can be provided by a team of four employees versus the current five employee team; this is an incremental savings that will be experienced over time as four employees will be on the payroll versus five. Another challenge that often falls within the Service Operation's realm is whether the organization is being reactive or proactive in its response to day to day operations of the IT infrastructure.

Regarding an organization's service operations, they can have either a reactive or proactive focus. A reactive organization does not act until some sort of stimulus compels the organization or individual to do so. For example, a Service Desk technician working in the network operations department (OPS) may be monitoring the organization's network health using software tools. The technician may not do anything until an alert is displayed on the screen. At that point, the technician may react by documenting the anomaly and initiating procedures to correct the problem. A proactive organization/individual is always looking for ways to improve the current situation. In a proactive environment, that same technician mentioned above may be monitoring network bandwidth and making data traffic adjustments to ensure no one path gets overly congested with traffic which would cause a problem. This is the act of being proactive in the service operations arena.

Although there is nothing inherently wrong with an organization being solely reactive in nature, but usually proactive behavior is viewed more positively because it enables the organization to keep a competitive advantage in an ever changing environment. One concept to keep in mind is that an organization that has chosen to be overly proactive can incur considerably more costs than one which is more reactively focused.   Often a balance must be reached between affordability and either reactive or proactive operations.

The processes aligned to ITIL's V3 Service Operation phase of the lifecycle are all aimed to provide structure to the operations of the IT services being provided to the business/customer by the IT provider.   Those processes include; Incident Management, Problem Management, Access Management, Event Management, & Request Fulfillment.   Perhaps the most visible process to the end user is Incident Management and will be addressed next.

Incident Management

The Incident Management process handles all incidents of an organization. Incidents may be failures, questions, or queries submitted by organizational users or technical staff to a service desk, or observed through the use of specialized monitoring software.   An incident is defined as an unplanned disruption to an IT service or a reduction in the quality of that service.   The primary objective of Incident management is to resume the regular state of affairs as quickly as possible and to minimize the impact on business processes (van Bon, et al., A Management Guide: Service Operation based on ITIL V3, 2008).

Incident management entails much more than simply responding to network outages.   A Service Desk is often the function within an IT department that "owns" all incidents for an organization.   The process flow for handling incidents will be briefly explained here based on a flowchart that appears in the book, *IT Service Management: A Guide for ITIL V3 Foundation Exam Candidates* (Brewster, Griffiths, Lawes, & Sansbury, 2010).   The Incident Management flowchart is included in the Appendix for reference.

An Incident is usually elevated by means of a user phone call to the Service Desk, a web user interface ticket created by a user/customer, or from event management software that illustrates an outage of some kind. An incident is not handled until it is known to exist. This is the incident identification step. Next, the incident must be logged (or registered). This is where a ticket is created in an outage tracking system (such as Remedy or Seibel, for example) to document all relevant information related to the outage. Categorizing the incident is the next step which may highlight what type of incident has occurred. Categories may be based upon the different type of networks or equipment that is used within the organization. Often how incidents are categorized varies by organization. Priority of the incident must be addressed based on urgency and impact the incident has on the organization. Priority levels 1 through 4 are often used with 1 being most severe or a major incident. Initial diagnosis occurs when the service desk technician tries to establish what went wrong and how it should be corrected. At this point the technician must determine if the incident can be corrected at their level or whether it must be escalated to a high skilled technician or engineer for resolution. This is called functional escalation. Depending on the level of business impact, management escalation may also be necessary. Regardless of which entity corrects the problem, the next step is resolution and recovery where a normal operational state returns and the service desk technician will resolve or close the incident record.

Incident management is a critical component of Service Operation's efforts to maintain the steady state of normal business operations by resolving issues as quickly as possible by virtually any means necessary. However, in most cases during incident management the underlying cause of the incident is not directly addressed. This is where Problem Management takes over.

Problem Management

The objective of problem management is to prevent problems and incidents, eliminate repeated incidents and minimize the impact of incidents that cannot be prevented. A problem is defined as the cause of one or more incidents. As an example to differentiate between incidents and problems take a group of e-mail servers that always seem to lock up once a day. Calls from e-mail users to the Service Desk would generate incidents where the Service Desk personnel may use a workaround for this known error to correct the problem. In this example, perhaps it is to reboot the servers. E-mail servers are now back in operation and the incidents can be closed.

This does not address the underlying reason why these servers lock up daily. Remember that Incident Management's goal to return to normal operation as soon as possible by virtually any means necessary. Incident Management has done its job. Problem Management is now needed to address the reason these servers have this persistent and repetitive issue. A Problem Management ticket may be generated and assigned to a network engineer to work. In our example, perhaps the engineer may discover that the servers are running with corrupted code that is causing the problem. A change request would be generated to delete the old and update the new code on each server. Resolving this problem has an added benefit in that the previous "daily" incidents on these servers would be eliminated and making the organization's e-mail service more reliable and robust.

As soon as a problem solution is found it should be applied to the problem to resolve it. But care should be taken to insure the solution does not negatively impact other services. This is where the Change Management process can play a part in the problem solution implementation to help insure that correcting one problem does not inadvertently create others. As should be understood, Problem

Management is greatly dependent on an effective Incident Management process to help identify problems; based on reported incidents, as quickly as possible.

Access Management

ITIL's Access Management could have very easily been included in the Information Security Management process discussed earlier in this book due to the security implications of granting IT access to users. However, it is equally appropriate to discuss Access Management within the context of the Service Operation phase of the lifecycle since in most organizations it is the operations personnel that are performing the tasks to grant network access to authorized users.

Access Management (often referred to as Identity Management) is viewed by many as an IT enabler for an organization because without the granting of access to users of IT services, IT would be of little use to the business (Casassa Mont, Beres, Pym, & Shiu, 2010). Traditionally there are 5 activities that take place during this process (van Bon, et al., A Management Guide: Service Operation based on ITIL V3, 2008): Verification, Granting Rights, Monitoring ID Status, Registering and Monitoring Access, and Revoking and Limiting Rights.

Verification addresses two questions; is the person requesting access who they claim to be; and does that person have a legitimate right to the service they are requesting? Granting rights in Access Management is just the act of executing the access policy established during Service Strategy. Access Management does not get to decide who receives access to what service. Monitoring identity is an important activity of the process because often someone's role will change over time which will impact their access level to some services. For example, some organizations have "privileged user" access which requires those employees to recertify yearly. Those that do not must have their special access terminated. Registering and monitoring is needed to ensure that the access granted is being used properly. Access Management is also responsible for limiting or revoking access when warranted. It is important to note that Access Management does not make the decision to terminate access for an employee, but simply carries out the directive when given. A good example would be regarding a terminated employee. It would be vital to ensure their accesses to company resources are revoked once they are no longer employed by the organization. Management of user access to organizational IT services is a strategically important component of Service Operation.

Event Management

During the course of discussing Service Operation, often terms like Incident, Problem, Request, and now Events tend to blend together. Prior to discussing yet another process, it may be advisable to distinguish between the terms based on definitions provided in a white paper by the IT Service Management Forum (Dugmore & Taylor, 2008):

Many international standards refer to a broad-based category of "defects" or similar terms. However, ITIL V3 draws a more detailed distinction:

Events: Neither defects nor requests, but actions that are monitored in order to detect deviations from normal behavior referred to as exceptions.

Incidents: Defects that have degraded or disrupted services, that are managed so that there is the minimum of business impact. This may not actually resolve the underlying defect.

Problems: Root cause analysis to identify and resolve incidents that have occurred and the prevention of potential defects.

Requests: These are typically small, low risk changes that can be dealt with in timescales similar to problems and incidents.

Event Management is the process that monitors all events that occur through the IT infrastructure. It allows for normal operation and detects and escalates exception conditions that happen on the network/infrastructure. Events are usually notifications that are created by an IT service, configuration item (router, switch, computer, server, etc.) or a monitoring tool. So that all aspects of Service Operation remain effective, an organization needs to be aware of the status of its networking infrastructure and be able to detect deviations to a normal or expected state.

In today's technologically advanced age, there are many event monitoring tools offered by a number of vendors to help organizations with their Event Management efforts. Most of these event management tools allow the organization to customize particular IT service states as to when a situation constitutes an event. For example, if a network circuit (IT service) between two locations is monitored to ensure the connection remains up and available for data traffic, the monitoring tool can be set up to produce an event only if a predetermined number of Ping messages across the path of the circuit fail.

The same tool can be designed to produce various levels of alerts. In regards to the example listed above perhaps the first time a ping message failed, an Informational event is generated. A second consecutive ping failure might generate a Warning event and subsequent ping failure would garner an Exception Event. To aid the Operations staff (likely the Service Desk) often color codes can be assigned to the types of events displayed within the monitoring tool. Informational could be coded as purple, Warning as yellow, and an Exception event would be red. This is helpful so the operations staff know exactly when to take action on an event. Based on policy established in Service Strategy and Design, Informational events may require no action whereas Warnings and Exception events require the operations staff to create a trouble ticket (essentially an Incident) and escalate the ticket to the network shop to begin troubleshooting the issue.

Perhaps the greatest benefit to the business that Event Management provides is the early detection of IT service incidents. Another benefit that can be realized in the use of some of the Event Management tools is the automated nature of the tool. Often these tools allow for automatic notification when an Exception event is detected so that management or technical personnel are notified via phone, text, or e-mail immediately when it occurs. Additionally, most allow the creation of a trouble ticket automatically. Event Management may only have indirect value to the business that employs the process, but most organizational leadership value the process since its value is in the processes ability to reveal the status of the organization's IT services.

Request Fulfillment

ITIL V3 uses the term service request as a generic reference for the requests that users submit to the IT department or service provider. A service request is a request from a user for information, advice, a standard change, or access to a service. These requests usually involve low risk type of service request. Because these requests occur often and involve very little risk to the business as a whole, it is recommended that they are handled in a separate ITIL process. Examples of user requests that are handled in the Request Fulfillment process include simple user password resets, requests for new computer software, request for access to an IT service, or any number of routine/low risk requests. Since most of these requests are repetitive in nature from the users in the workforce, the workflow to respond to these types of requests is normally already pre-determined and usually easily fulfilled.

The below figure illustrates the process used by organizations to fulfill these types of requests:

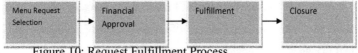

Figure 10: Request Fulfillment Process

Menu Request Selection is the step where the user can make the request, usually from a predefined menu on an organizational website. For example, many United States federal agencies have an internal web site which allows users to submit low risk IT requests. There are usually financial obligations to filling these types of requests, so most of these requests require supervisor or a manager's approval prior to the request being filled. Once the request is provided to the user, the operations staff (usually the Service Desk) will resolve or close the service request ticket that generated the request.

With the strategy used to ensure the services meet the needs of the business; the design of those services and the careful transition into the operational environment of those services, it is during operations where the organization begins to recognize the benefits of the IT services they have procured. However, the ITIL lifecycle does not end here. It is often during the Service Operation phase of the lifecycle when it is discovered that changes can be made to a service or process that can be of benefit to service users, IT provider, or the business. Continual Service Improvement is the fifth and final phase of the ITIL V3 lifecycle and will be discussed in the next section.

Continual Service Improvement

Everything is worthy of improvement at some point in its lifecycle. In the 1980s and earlier, if someone wished to compose a letter or write a story; they often would turn to a typewriter to complete the task. An argument could easily be made that a personal computer with a word processing program installed is nothing more than an improvement on the typewriter. Many years ago the primary mode of transportation was the horse and buggy. The improvement on the horse and buggy was the horseless carriage; otherwise known as the automobile. The point being made is that all things outlive their useful purpose and must be changed, adapted, or improved upon to remain in a useful state. This is as true for IT services as it is for the products that we use every day.

IT services exist in order to support the business. So IT services must align and re-align to the changing business needs by making improvements to the IT services that support and often sustain the business strategy. This service improvement is such a critical aspect of ITIL, the concept is considered the fifth and final phase of the ITIL V3 lifecycle.

Continual Service Improvement (CSI) and organizational change are closely tied because in order to make continual improvements a change in organizational mentality is often required. Many CSI initiatives fail because they are unable to achieve this cultural change; and being unable to do so we are stuck in the status quo without the ability to achieve needed improvements. John P. Kotter, Professor of Leadership at the Harvard Business School, examined over a hundred companies and discovered eight crucial steps needed to successfully change an organization. These steps are illustrated below (van Bon, et al., A Management Guide: Continual Service Improvement based on ITIL V3, 2008):

--Create a Sense of Urgency—ask the question "what happens if we do nothing at all and keep that status quo?"

--<u>Form a coalition</u>—usually one person cannot change an entire organization. A small key team with the proper authority and resources can begin making the change.

--<u>Create a vision</u>—a good organizational vision helps to create a goal and purpose for CSI.

--<u>Communicate the vision</u>—all stakeholders should understand the vision; putting together a communications plan can help

--<u>Empower others to act on the vision</u>—remove obstacles and provide clear direction by setting attainable goals. Supply people with the resources they need.

--<u>Plan for and create quick wins</u>—determine what small improvements can be made quickly and successfully. Communicate these successes to the team to build added support

--<u>Consolidate improvements and create more change</u>-- quick wins motivate; medium term improvements provide confidence in the organization's ability to effect change.

--<u>Institutionalize the change</u>—Make change acceptance the norm in the organization by:

-Hiring employees with experience in the field of IT management.

-From the outset of a change improvement initiative, utilize work instructions to provide clarity.

-Set up a training effort to provide IT management training.

-Integrate new IT solutions and projects with existing processes.

As will be discussed further in this book, for most an ITIL implementation will not work well if a "big bang" approach is attempted. That same approach usually will not work when attempting to create an improvement initiative within an organization. For this reason, this is essentially why Dr. W. Edwards Deming developed a step-by-step approach to improvement. This is the Plan-Do-Check-Act (PDCA) approach that is illustrated in the figure below (Zwetsloot, 2003).

Figure 11. Basic Deming Improvement Cycle (Zwetsloot, 2003).

The Deming model can be equally applied to aid in implementing an improvement process within an organization or to make improvements within already existing IT services within an organization. The latter is where the primary ITIL focus will be. When PDCA is used in conjunction with continual improvement of processes and services, the focus is more on the "check" and "act" steps. There are some activities in the "plan" and "do" steps that are addressed; these just are not the primary focus.

When planning improvement initiatives with IT services, goals must be set at the very outset to ensure everyone understands the desired end state. Additionally, expected gaps anticipated in attaining the goal must be identified and addressed if possible. In the "do" step, it is important to provide a smooth execution of the process and to eliminate as many obstacles and discrepancies as possible. During the "check" step of the PDCA, implemented service improvements are compared to the measures of success established during the "plan" phase. The comparison determines if a gap exists between the improvement objectives and the operational process state. The expected output from the "check" stage is a recommendation for an improvement. The "act" step requires the implementing of the actual service and service management improvements. Project decisions at this stage serve as the input for the next round of the Plan-Do-Check-Act cycle, closing the loop as input to the next "plan" step (Case & Spalding, 2007).

Service Improvement

Service Improvement process is best explained by discussing the 7-Step Improvement Process illustrated in the figure below:

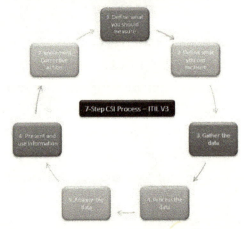

Figure 12: 7-Step Improvement Process (Bhardwah, 2009).

Step 1—Define What You Should Measure

Deciding what to measure should be a collaborative effort. The business, customers, and the IT provider should input ideas as to what data should be captured. Using the Service Catalog is a good place to start to see what may be viable data to measure. Compile a list that is driven by business requirements (remember IT supports the business vision, strategy, and goals). Do not try to list every single conceivable measurable concept. The "should measure" list can get lengthy very quickly.

Step 2—Define What You Can Measure

Just because an organization feels they should measure something, does not mean the organization has the ability or resources to do so. Every organization may find that there are some limitations and restrictions on what can be measures. For example, if an organization wanted to measure how many phone calls came into their Service Desk over a period of time, without an Automated Call Distribution (ACD) phone system that could capture this data, it would be nearly impossible to measure with a Plain Old Telephone System (POTS).

Step 3—Gather the Data

Gathering data requires some form of monitoring to be in place. Monitoring can be in the form of technology tools and applications or even a manual process for some tasks. Gathering bandwidth utilization over a circuit path would require a network monitoring tool such as Computer Associates (CA) eHealth to capture this data.

Step 4—Process the Data

Monitoring tools often do not generate data that is all that useable or understandable to the audience it is intended. If the data was taken directly from the gathering stage and presented to an audience, it may not make much sense to them if presented in a raw format. Data may be output from the gathering stage as numbers, percentages, dates, etc. Compiling this in a visually appealing manner is useful for the understanding of the intended audience.

Step5—Analysing the Data

This is the "So what" stage. For example, after the data is processed and a visually appealing chart is developed that shows the Service Desk has a trend of reduced call volumes over the last three months. What does that data mean? It could mean that the organization is experiencing fewer Incidents (good). Or, it could mean that the Service Desk personnel are so inept at helping customers, service users have just given up calling the Service Desk at all; and have found other means of resolving their issues (very bad).   A deep dive into the data (analyze) is vital to ensure that the data is fully understood.

Step 6—Presenting and Using the Data

Using the example above, assume it is that the Service Desk personnel are less than proficient in their abilities. This data would be presented to an audience (presumably a senior manager or the service desk manager) with the findings of reduced calls and the unfortunate reasons for the fewer than anticipated call volume.

Step 7—Implementing Corrective Measures

Lastly, the newfound wisdom would be used to make corrective actions or optimize the less than desirable state. In our example, perhaps the service desk manager would deduce that all (or most) of the service desk technicians were in need of additional customer service skills training. Presumably, after the training and as the word of better customer service from the Service Desk spread across the organization, call volumes would begin to return to a more expected level.

Service Reporting

This is the process responsible for the generation and supply of the reports of the results achieved by improvement efforts. All stakeholders (customers, IT provider, and the business) should agree on the type of reports to be generated, frequency, and the content of the reports. The initial step in Service Reporting is the gathering of data that was addressed previously.

IT departments often gather a great deal of data, all of which many not be all that interesting or of value to the business. So, at this step of Service Reporting it is important to fully understand the target group that will receive the report(s), as knowing this will help in guiding the collection of data to that which will be of the highest value to the target audience.

In processing the data keep in mind that the business is often interested in data presented in a historical overview format. The reason for this is that often the business is interested in events from the past that may impact the business today or into the future. Additionally, business leaders are concerned how these events may impact the performance of the business and how IT will use the data to mitigate potential threats.

The next step of the process is to publish the report to all applicable stakeholders. Fine tune the report for the applicable target group. Generally speaking, there are three target groups that often receive some type of service report: The Business, Senior IT management, and Internal IT department. Consider the data group if it is important to the target group in regards to what information is presented to them. For example, the business may not understand or even care that a service's availability was 93% available during the last month. That figure may have little meaning. They may simply want to know how long was the service unavailable to the users of the service (20 minutes on X day, 30 minutes on X day, etc.). Additionally, from a business perspective, the concern is all about the service. In most organizational situations the report should be structured to present data from an agreed service level perspective; and not equipment or device specific. Reports at that granular of a level will be of little use to the organizational leaders (the business).

Service Measurement

Service Measurement is the process within CSI that helps to address the question, "what is it that we should measure?" The challenge that many organizations face is the creation of a Service Measurement Framework that leads to value-added reporting (Case & Spalding, 2007). Perhaps the most important step in creating a Service Measurement Framework is to fully understand the business processes and to capture those that are most critical to bringing value to the business. Recall that the IT goals and objectives must support the goals and objectives of the business. Understanding this, the focus on what to measure can be more defined.

One might think that Service Measurement is about looking at the past (capturing past events in a historical manner). Although this is true enough; the underlying reason for doing so is to focus on the future. The adage, "you cannot know where you are going, unless you know where you have been" is indicative of the concept. Data is captured from the past so it can be analyzed with an eye to the future with the goal of how to do things better and improve upon the lessons learned from the past.

Building a Service Management Framework means deciding which of the following need to be monitored and measured:

--Services

--Components

--Service Management processes that support the services

--Activities within the processes

--Outputs

It is often best to select a balanced approach in determining which of the above to measure. Selecting a combination of these may be the best method. However, it is important to understand that availability of resources may prevent an organization from being this all encompassing. Again, it really comes down to what is fundamentally important to the business. An organization that values e-mail as a service, may wish to monitor the e-mail service and ALL the components that make up that service. Perhaps overkill for some organizations, but for others it is where their value lies.

CSI is the phase of the lifecycle that ensures that IT continues to support the business even when the business goals and vision may change. Without CSI as part of the ITIL lifecycle, eventually IT services would soon fall out of favor because they did not stay in step with the business objectives and goals. Once IT fails to support the business, it no longer provides any value and becomes a waste of business investment.

With ITIL V3 fully addressed, it is time to move on to the focus of the following sections—implementing ITIL within a U. S. government agency. Having a skilled and trained ITIL workforce is fundamental in being able to address the challenges in an ITIL implementation. The next section will address ITIL certification and training options for the government workforce.

ITIL Training & Certification

How a Trained Workforce Aids Implementation

Whenever an organization (public or private) initiates any implementation effort that will impact the entire organization it is critical that there are specific area experts available to lead and work the implementation. This is as true for a government agency's efforts in implementing ITIL as it is in an automotive manufacturer's efforts in designing a new car model. In order to be successful in both ventures, each organization needs experts in these areas (ITIL and automotive design).

An expert is usually someone that has a prolonged experience through practice and/or education in a particular field (Wikipedia the free encyclopedia, 2012). A government agency can acquire this expert ITIL knowledge via two distinct paths. The agency can look internally for employees that either have the required skills to aid in an ITIL implementation (or can be trained so they can possess the needed knowledge and skills), or the agency can look to outside contractors that can be contractually hired to provide this expertise. There are benefits to both options. If the business has the financial resources to hire external contractors (good ones can be costly), this may immediately establish the expertise needed for the organization. Taking the time to cultivate internal experts would likely have a more lasting effect for the agency.

Implementing ITIL within any government agency can take some time to fully accomplish. For this reason, many government agencies may find it more to their advantage to cultivate internal expertise so this knowledge is available for an extended period of time at a more affordable cost. Since an ITIL implementation for a government agency can take considerable time to fully implement (depending on the level of implementation) this is why an ITIL trained workforce can aid the implementation efforts. It is a reasonable assumption that agency employees are on the payroll regardless, so to provide some level of training within the ITIL arena would likely be the better long term solution. Contracting to bring an ITIL expert with the needed experience may still prove a valuable short term option for the agency. However, it is still a better long term option to invest in the agency employees that understand the agency strategy, goals, and objectives. An external ITIL expert, may know ITIL, but certainly will not have the breadth of agency knowledge and experience that many agency employees possess. Once an agency embraces the fact that their own employees are the key to a successful ITIL implementation, the next step is to assess the current ITIL skill set within the organization and what ITIL training needs currently exist and how to meet those training needs.

How to Train a Workforce

Training employees in ITIL processes has become a necessity, if not for basic employee awareness, then for greater needs that may include the fact that some employees of the agency may be directly involved in an ITIL implementation initiative. There are a few options available to ensure employees receive ITIL training. The first and often more costly option is to solicit outside trainers to train an entire workforce. Today, many consulting firms offer ITIL training in response to the growing demand for ITIL certified staff (Cator-Steel & Toleman, 2007). Although costly, this method does have one underlying benefit. Hiring an outside training provider, such as Learning Tree or Global Knowledge, would likely ensure that all agency employees receive the same level of training as these vendors have established and approved training plans their instructors use regardless when or where the training takes place. For a government agency, often with employees spread across the globe, this can be an attractive option and worth the added expense if financial resources are available to support the effort.

With shrinking federal dollars, this is often not a feasible option for most government organizations. Agencies must adopt other training methods to better utilize the limited training resources available. One method that many organizations employ is to train a select few in a formal manner so they can return to the organization to train other employees. In the U. S. military this method was commonly referred to as "Train the Trainer." There are definite advantages to be had by training employees to train other employees. This is a strategy that can be applicable to other areas, in addition to ITIL. Teach employees to train and you will increase the effectiveness of your internal training. Employees are familiar with the workings – both good and bad – of your internal organization. They should be familiar with the goals, the culture or environment, the company strengths, the company weaknesses, and the actual employees. This gives employees an advantage over a trainer who has to learn about the culture, the company strengths, the company weaknesses, and also get to know the people (Heathfield, 2012). The benefit in the ITIL area is that a trainer for an ITIL Foundation level (introductory level of ITIL training) requires no special skills or approvals other than to hold a current ITIL Foundation level certification. The entire ITIL certification process will be discussed in detail in the next section. This method requires a greater ITIL training investment in a smaller number of agency employees; but once this small cadre of ITIL trainer/experts is fully qualified, the remainder of those that need ITIL training can be accomplished internally at a much reduced cost.

Although a government agency attempting any level of ITIL implementation will need some ITIL experts to be able to successfully lead the implementation, there is another option that can be used to train the remainder of the agency workforce without tying up the few ITIL experts in teaching foundation level courses to hundreds of fellow co-workers. Computer-based training (CBT) can be a cost effective training tool that can be more convenient to the overall workforce because employees are not locked into an ITIL Foundations classroom for a week or more. A CBT can be just as convenient a training option for the organization as a whole as it is for the individual employee. Since the employees are free to complete the ITIL CBT at their convenience often outside of normal duty hours, ITIL training for many employees need not disrupt the day to day operational duties of many of the agency employees. Additionally, those agency employees who were provided more costly and time consuming advanced ITIL training are free to utilize their advanced skills to engage and lead the agency's ITIL implementation efforts.

There are many ITIL training options for the government agency to choose from. Often a combination of external training, internal training, and computer based may be the best overall option for the agency. The ITIL strategy and goals plus available training resources will often play a deciding factor in which training options an agency deems appropriate. One aspect of ITIL training that has given it importance and sustainability for organizations is the industry accepted certification process that aligns to most of the available ITIL training courses. A workforce where most employees have attained an internationally recognized IT certification can benefit the organization in many ways; least of which is having more capable employees to serve the organization's customers. Understanding the ITIL certification process is a fundamental aspect of ITIL training and therefore important to an agency's ability to successfully implement ITIL within the agency.

ITIL Certification Process

As was previously addressed, ITIL has undergone many transformations since its inception. Since its launch it has undergone three versions and a "refresh" of the third version as recently as 2011. Along with the changes experienced with ITIL over the years, the certification process has also undergone changes. As recently as 2007 under ITIL V2, there were three certification levels available— Foundation, Practitioner, and Service Manager each progressing in difficulty and requiring a greater depth of understanding of the subject matter. With the emergence of the ITIL lifecycle concept in ITIL V3, the certification structure change as well. The Foundation level remained largely unchanged, but Practitioner was changed to Intermediate Level and Service Manager became Expert level. In early 2012, ITIL Master was released to describe the highest level of ITIL certification attainable. Additionally, a credit structure was set up to allow lower level courses to count toward attaining higher level certifications as depicted in the figure below:

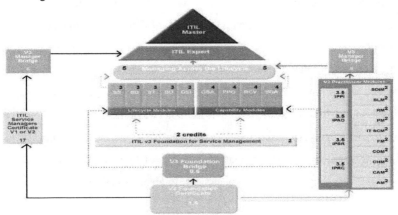

Figure 13: ITIL Certification Scheme (ITIL V3 Certification Scheme, 2012)

The figure above illustrates current V3 certification scheme and the V2 to V3 certification path. When V3 was adopted, a change in the certification scheme to assign credits to individual ITIL courses completed successfully to include previous V2 courses and exams passed. A previous holder of a V2 Foundation certificate (1.5 credits) could take a bridge course worth .5 credits and if successful be awarded a V3 Foundation certificate. Bridging from V2 to V3 is no longer an option as the bridging exams are no longer available. The figure above illustrates the path to V3 Expert (requiring 22 credits) was available to any holder of one or more V2 certifications. For example a V2 Service Manager would have been awarded 17 V3 credits. Completion of the V3 Manager's Bridging course/exam would garner another 5 credits; thereby attaining 22 credits and the ITIL V3 Expert distinction.

Currently, the path to ITIL V3 Expert is straightforward. Credits are awarded for courses taken and associated exams passed. The passing of the V3 Foundation exam (class room attendance is not required for this exam) is 2 credits. Credits awarded for course and exam completion for the Intermediate level is illustrated below:

Lifecycle Modules	Credits
Service Strategy (SS)	3
Service Design (SD)	3
Service Transition (ST)	3
Service Operation (SO)	3
Continual Service Improvement (CSI)	3

Capability Modules	
Planning, Protection, & Optimization (PPO)	4
Service Offerings & Agreements (SOA)	4
Operational Support & Analysis (OSA)	4
Release, Control, & Validation (RCV)	4

Figure 14: ITIL V3 Intermediate Level Modules

Any combination of these intermediate level courses/exams successfully passed in conjunction with Foundation (2 credits) and Managing Across the Lifecycle Course (5 credits) that earned the candidate at least 22 total credits would garner the candidate the ITIL V3 Expert certification. Recently a more advanced certification has been developed entitled ITIL Master.

To attain ITIL Master a candidate must possess an ITIL Expert certification. The Master certification does not require course attendance or successfully passing an exam. For the ITIL Master distinction, a candidate must write a paper detailing the use of ITIL principles in practical use and successfully defend the paper in an interview to a panel of other ITIL Master qualified practitioners.

Having an ITIL trained and certified workforce can be a critical component of a successful ITIL implementation strategy for the government agency. ITIL's certification scheme provides multiple levels of training and certification covering all aspects of ITIL V3 lifecycle and its processes. This flexibility allows the agency leadership various options in training and certifying their employees; from the basic Foundation level to the more advanced Expert and Master level certifications. Although the ITIL training and certification scheme offers many attractive options, this does not negate the fact that the government agency is faced with challenges and constraints in getting their employees ITIL trained and certified.

Governmental Training Constraints

Government agencies face unique training challenges that are not faced by the private organization. The diversity of the government agency workforce and legal and regulatory constraints are two of the primary training constraints faced by government agencies that private businesses do not encounter.

As opposed to private firms, the government agency is faced with addressing training needs for a variety of employee types (government civilians SES/GS/NAF, contractors and sub-contractors from multiple companies, military all branches, and various equipment and software vendors). With such a diverse workforce it makes it extremely difficult to develop any ITIL training program that can be universally applied to all agency workers. This is not a problem that most private organizations face. One of the greatest issues is the training funding. In most cases, training funding for government civilians cannot be used for military or contractor personnel located at the same agency. Additionally, contractor funding cannot be used for civilian or military personnel's ITIL training needs. Depending on how diverse the government agency is will often determine how many distinct training programs will exist (and need to be managed) by a single government agency.

Although agencies have always been allowed to administer their own training programs, the law, funding authority, and federal requirements must always be taken into consideration. Private businesses have much more freedom to administer their own internal training programs. Since government agencies are funded by taxpayer dollars, there is considerably more oversight in how agencies spend their allotted funds; to include agency training dollars. The most significant agency governance that all U. S. government agencies must adhere to regarding the training of their employees is the Government Employees Training Act (GETA). The act, passed in 1958, created the framework for agencies to plan, develop, establish, implement, evaluate, and fund training and development programs designed to improve the quality and performance of the workforce (OPM Training Policy Handbook, 2007). Title 5 United States Code deals with federal employee issues with chapter 41 specifically dealing with training of government employees. Along with GETA and the U. S. Code, often Presidential guidance would be issued by Executive Orders (EO). EO's provide agency heads with added presidential guidance on how the law should be used. Title 5 of the Code of Federal Regulations Part 410 addresses policy and specific requirements for training in government agencies (OPM Training Policy Handbook, 2007). The appendix illustrates this training governance in the Summary of Legal Foundation of Training.

All of these legal, legislative, and executive directives were put into place to ensure government agencies are held accountable for properly utilizing the country's taxpayer dollars. However, these federal directives, although necessary, complicate an agency's ability to develop and implement an ITIL training plan for their employees. Typically private businesses are not mandated to comply with such a vast array of legal requirements in order to implement a training program for their employees. This is yet another distinction between the government agency's path to ITIL implementation and that of the private firm.

Implementation Basics

One of the first tasks to implementing ITIL within an organization is to determine whether the agency can support a full scale or Big Bang implementation approach or must adopt a more phased approach based upon the process that may yield the greatest benefit for the government agency. Big Bang may have the biggest reward, but may also pose the greatest risk to the organization. A phased or "little bang" approach may offer less reward but pose a smaller risk to the organization.

Big Bang Approach

This approach is when all intended ITIL processes are implemented in unison. A government agency that has determined the need for Incident, Problem, Change, and Release Management process would begin the implementation of all process essentially at the same time if planning to utilize a big bang implementation approach. The benefit for this approach is that the most vital processes that the organization needs implemented will be accomplished much sooner than had there been a more phased or methodical approach. The drawbacks to such an approach are higher potential risks and greater costs.

To initiate multiple process implementation efforts at the same time requires greater manpower investment either current experienced employees or contractor personnel. Either way it will incur a significant financial burden for the agency. If significant agency employees are utilized to participate in the implementation effort, there is the risk that the agency's operational mission will suffer due to these operational staff being tasked to the implementation effort; thereby resulting in fewer employees designated to perform the day to day duties of the agency.

A government agency must seriously consider all benefits of such an implementation and weigh those benefits against the possible risks of such an effort. If the determination is that the risks outweigh the possible benefits of an "all at once" ITIL process implementation, another implementation option is available.

Phased Approach

A more cautious and measured ITIL implementation approach is the phased approach. This approach may also be called the mini-bang approach. Where ITIL is concerned, a systematic method would be employed to determine which ITIL process, if properly implemented within the organization, would yield the greatest benefit. As is the case with the Big Bang approach, there are benefits and risks to the phased approach as well.

Any measured implementation approach is likely to produce results that are also more measured in overall impact to the agency. Any agency that took 6 months to implement an ITIL Change Management process would experience only the direct benefits attributable to the newly instituted change process. From an organizational perspective, a new change process may not directly impact all aspects of the organization; and for many employees may go virtually unnoticed. If further process implementations are attempted, agency leadership would need to advertise previous ITIL successes to garner further support for other ITIL initiatives.

The most significant benefit to this approach is the cost reductions and ability to utilize manpower resources more efficiently. Recall from the "Training and Certification" section of this discussion that resourcing the ITIL training needs of the workforce can be a challenge and often only a select few employees can be trained to the level needed to engage and lead an ITIL implementation. To this end, a phased approach can focus these highly skilled ITIL experts in the implementation of one process at a time versus spreading their talents across multiple process implementations at the same time. For the U. S. government agency, which option is usually the best?

U. S. Government Agency—Phased Approach is often the best option

Government agencies are often vast organizations that are involved in a multitude of activities that encompass the day to day operational endeavors of the organization; particularly at the federal level. Essentially, this results in an organization that is involved in many significant projects simultaneously that utilize not only human capital to accomplish the tasks but also the dwindling financial resources needed to accomplish the projects. Any "resource-intensive" initiatives the agency is undergoing; from a datacenter renovation or other IT infrastructure upgrade to a process driven implementation such as COBIT or a Six Sigma effort, must seriously consider a phased ITIL implementation.   In John Wallhoff's article "Combining ITIL with COBIT and 17799," he reinforces this concept in saying, "Another recommendation that is repeated in any article, book, or presentation we have come across on this issue is that you shall not go for complete implementation of ITIL, COBIT, and ISO 17799 at the same time. A big bang implementation is bound to fail. The difficult task is instead to choose issues that are important to you, from a cost/benefit, risk mitigation or regulatory compliance perspective." (Wallhoff, 2004).

The big bang implementation approach is not recommended for any organization that is actively involved in multiple large scale implementations of any kind. For most U. S. government agencies which often find the need to reinvent themselves in efforts to save taxpayer dollars while continuing to provide the same levels of service; this phased implementation concept is particularly applicable.

Overcoming Constraints and Risks

Much of the inherent constraints and risks of an ITIL implementation undertaken by a government entity can be controlled or mitigated by the selection of the phased implementation approach. This is not to suggest that selecting the phased approach will eliminate any implementation constraints or risks; certainly this should not be the expected outcome of utilizing the phase approach over the big bang method. But the phased approach will allow the agency to better deal with the unexpected when it does arise.

A number of risks and constraints in implementing ITIL were identified by Wan & Liang in a recently published paper; and the following root risk factors are of particular importance to the government agency (Wan & Liang, 2012).

- Objectives of the implementation effort are not clear.
- Inadequate or ineffective communication to the staff members.
- Senior members do not give proper priority to the project.
- Business strategy of the enterprise is vague.
- Brain Drain on the organization is too great.
- IT infrastructure planning and design in the enterprise is unreasonable.

The risks and constraints for the government agency can be as endless and all encompassing as that of the private firm. The key for the government agency is the use of the phased approach to aid in controlling and managing those risks.

Agency Benefits

The greatest agency benefit of using the phased approach is the reduction of risks and the ability to control those risks that remain. Utilization of the phased approach minimizes the impact of those risks when they do occur. If it were decided to implement only Incident Management, this ITIL process would likely only impact certain segments of the agency. If things didn't go well due to an unforeseen or uncontrolled risk or constraint; the impacted segment of the agency would be smaller and more controllable than had the big bang approach been undertaken where multiple processes and numerous agency components were involved in the implementations.

Once the government agency embraces the idea that the phased approach is the best ITIL implementation option; utilization of the phased approach to select the ITIL process or processes that benefit the goals and vision or the agency can begin in earnest. A U. S. government agency must fully understand their vision and strategy and how they serve their customer base. This is the first step in a government agency being able to use the phased approach to begin its ITIL implementation.

ITIL Implementation within a U. S. Government Agency

For the government agency, realizing the need to implement ITIL into their business processes may be an easy decision for the agency leadership. Deciding where to start with the limited resources to implement ITIL is often the more challenging question. ITIL V3 does not lend itself to provide a definitive starting point due to the lifecycle approach. On the surface this fact may not seem to be favorable to the agency leader looking for guidance to start the implementation. The lifecycle approach is aimed at managing the lifecycle of a service, and therefore processes need not be implemented in a particular order. This means that it is not necessary to start at page one of the Service Strategy volume and continue until the final page of the Continual Service Improvement book (Fry, 2010).

This lack of definitive implementation guidance is often viewed as a drawback to ITIL V3, but the reality is that the freedom to implement ITIL in any manner that benefits the agency is actually a positive aspect of Version 3. The problem that the agency faces is although there is freedom to start the implementation with any ITIL process; which process is the right process to implement for the agency? This section will provide guidance for the U. S. government agency to use in selecting the ITIL process that has the highest probability for the best return on their investment. This process, graphically illustrated in the appendix in Figure A5, will begin with the agency's full and complete understanding of their agency vision, mission, and strategy.

Understanding the Agency's Vision, Mission, and Strategy

Any government agency, regardless whether it is at the federal, state, or local levels, must have a full understanding of their agency vision and strategy. Basically, any government agency must understand why the agency exists in the first place and how and what segments of the population it exists to serve. Failure of any government agency to fully embrace its identity and mission to the people that it serves will certainly cause any significant project implementation to be a challenging undertaking. A government agency that believes its fundamental mission is one thing, but reality dictates that their mission is something quite different, may undergo an exhaustive research effort to determine which ITIL process would yield the greatest ROI only to discover that the process implemented failed to do so.

An example would be an agency that believes its fundamental mission is to manage government network security intrusions (Information Security Management) and implement that ITIL process. The failure being that the networks that the agency provides security on are used by their customers. An avenue for their customers to interact with the agency, regarding network outages and intrusions, may prove a better return on the agency's investment in an ITIL implementation (Incident Management/Service Desk), if not already in place. This is the classic example of an agency "believing" that their mission is to serve the "technology" that helps support their mission rather than the customers that use the networks that the agency protects. So, from the very outset, it is critical that the agency have a realistic understanding of their primary reasons for existence and who they exist to serve. Once this is embraced, the next step toward an educated and informed ITIL implementation is the identification of the agency critical tasks.

Critical Tasks

If a government agency believes that they have a clear understanding of their mission, vision, and strategy, they need to investigate how this is accomplished. The most fundamental method is an examination of the work being performed by the agency employees. U. S. government employees often have established training records that detail the tasks that they are required to remain proficient on in the performance of their duties. Certainly some government agencies may contain thousands of employees and to examine each employee's training records would take considerable effort to accomplish. The fact is that it would be counterproductive to fully examine every task that every employee performs to assess the critical nature of that individual employee task. Realistically, it would be found that many employees perform the same identical tasks and likely only certain tasks could be deemed "impactful" to the mission of the agency.

For example, if a U. S. government agency has a network operations center that performs network health monitoring and is staffed by 45-50 agency employees that provide 24/7 coverage; it is conceivable that each of these employees perform the same day to day tasks. There would be no reason to gather the same data from 50 employees if it was already known that the results would yield 50 identical samples. Additionally, many of the tasks agency employees perform may have minimal or no impact on the overall mission of the agency. Although all tasks an employee performs and becomes qualified to do will yield some level of benefit, all employee tasks are not mission impacting and therefore not considered Agency Critical Tasks.

What are the agency's critical tasks? In an article on mindtools.com, critical tasks are described as "work that is at the core or the organization's performance" (Aligning the Drivers of High Performance, 2012). These are the agency tasks performed by the employees that define the ultimate mission of the agency. This is the most important work being performed at the agency that aligns with the strategy, vision, and mission of the organization. The agency employees are those that perform these agency critical tasks based upon work they have been trained to accomplish, aligned to their applicable training plan.

Agency Employees, Critical Tasks, and the Training Plan

Agency employees are at the cornerstone of what is required to ensure the agency accomplishes its mission. Employees must be professional and dedicated to the mission of their agency, competent to perform the duties of their position (trained and qualified), and in some cases certified to perform those tasks. Within most U. S. government agencies, due to the critical nature of the work being performed in most of these organizations, it is vital that these critical tasks (and other tasks for that matter) are standardized in their performance regardless which employee performs them. This is where the training plan can provide benefits. Most agencies maintain some type of training program to ensure their employees acquire and maintain the needed skills to perform their duties. There are numerous benefits to such a training program as addressed by Carl Duncker, a training consultant specializing in the delivery of efficient and effective training solutions to the public and private business sectors. In an article, he lists 5 business benefits of a training program with one of the benefits being the maintenance of quality and standardization of training tasks. Mr. Duncker's benefits are illustrated below (Duncker, 2006):

--Impact on the bottom line--Successful employee training delivers improvements in employee performance which, in turn, creates a better performing business and an improved bottom line.

--Staff retention—A good training program improves employee retention, reducing resources needed for recruitment and retraining of new hires

--Improved productivity and quality--Training that meets both staff and employer needs can increase the quality and flexibility of a business's services by fostering: accuracy and efficiency, good work safety practices, and improved customer services. With standardized training procedures for tasks, the quality and uniformity of these tasks will be identical regardless of which agency employee performs the tasks.

--The flow-on effect—training benefits experienced in one section of an organization will be experienced in other parts of the organization.

--Remaining competitive--Businesses must continually change their work practices and infrastructure to stay competitive in a global market. Training staff to manage the implementation of business strategies, improvements to procedures and customer service policies can also act as a benchmark for future recruitment and quality assurance practices.

Being able to standardize training tasks through the use of an established agency (or agency section) training plan is important in the performance of the critical tasks of the agency. With the agency mission, vision, and strategy established along with the critical tasks performed by agency employees; the remaining process to aid the government agency in its efforts to implement the best ITIL process(s) based on highest probable ROI; will use a fictitious case study example for clarity.

CASE STUDY

The Defense Information Systems Agency (DISA) is an agency of the Department of Defense which provides command and control to war-fighters worldwide. DISA's VISION is "Information Superiority in defense of the nation. Their MISSION is "DISA, a Combat Support Agency, provides, operates, and assures command and control, information sharing capabilities, and a globally accessible enterprise information infrastructure in direct support to joint war-fighters, National level leaders, and other mission and coalition partners across the full spectrum of operations" (DISA Vision and Mission, 2012).

Since DISA is charged with managing a network infrastructure to provide communications and command and control to war-fighters worldwide, DISA has a Network Operations Center (NOC) that monitors and provides tracking and troubleshooting for this vast network infrastructure of circuits. This NOC is manned 24/7 with nearly 50 employees all trained to perform the same mission following the same procedures as outlined in an approved NOC Training Plan. DISA leadership believes that ITIL best practice can help to improve the efficiencies of the NOC and wish to initiate an implementation but are uncertain how to begin based on the limited resources (due to federal budgetary constraints) available for such a project.

In the remainder of this section, it will be illustrated how DISA leadership can use the critical tasks being performed by NOC employees along with a categorizing technique to select the ITIL process(s) that when implemented will provide the greatest return on DISA's ITIL investment.

Categorizing of Employee Tasks

Prior to categorizing the critical tasks, the first step is to pull those tasks out of the DISA NOC's training plan. As referenced prior, since duties and responsibilities of all 50 NOC employees are identical, the training tasks in each employee's training record should also be identical. All that is being captured is the critical tasks that the NOC performs, so for this data capture taking one of the employees training records and pulling the critical tasks out of that record. Employee training records could be stored in folders in a file cabinet within the NOC or stored electronically on a SharePoint site. Any manner that allows them to be accessible to the employee and trainer/supervisor so the records can be maintained and updated as needed is a sufficient storage method. For the benefit of this case study example, the exercise of reviewing the training record reveals the following Critical Tasks that the DISA NOC employees perform:

> *Equipment shipping procedures*
>
> *Familiarity with NOC Standard Operating Procedures*
>
> *Familiarity with NOC Service Level Agreements*
>
> *Familiarity with NOC Operational Level Agreements*
>
> *Ability to manipulate data on the NOC portal*
>
> *Manage network bandwidth/availability and capacity*
>
> *Alt route circuits and services*
>
> *Document network outages in ticket tracking system*
>
> *Ability to use Network Monitoring Tools*
>
> *Ability to access routers on the networks and correct anomalies*
>
> *Ability to access switches on the networks and correct anomalies*
>
> *Ability to access cryptographic equipment on the networks and correct anomalies*
>
>   *Sub-task--Manage via Encryption Manager Software*
>
> *Ability to research site information using existing NOC database*
>
> *Able to make daily network health checks*
>
> *Able to ping/trace route network components to test connectivity*

With the NOC critical tasks identified from data in the NOC training plan, it is now time to identify and define some categories to place these tasks into. Task categories can be anything that distinctively delineates the functions of the tasks. For this case study, Malcolm Fry's example of RESOURCE, ACTION, UNDERPINNING, and INFLUENCING (Fry, 2010) will be used as our categories. First there must be definition to these categories.

Resource Tasks—these are tasks that ensure that the necessary resources are available to support the mission of the organization/department.

Action Tasks—These are tasks of an operational nature performed as part of an organization's efforts to maintain normal functionality.

Underpinning Tasks—These are supporting tasks that underpin other tasks.

Influencing Tasks—These tasks modify and influence the way the action tasks are performed.

It is now possible to align the critical tasks into these categories. This part of the process requires an understanding of the critical tasks identified that the NOC performs; so this may require further input from NOC leaders if a task is not completely understood. Once this process is completed the results should reveal the following.

*Equipment shipping procedures—**Resource or Underpinning***

*Familiarity with NOC Standard Operating Procedures--**Influencing***

*Familiarity with NOC Service Level Agreements--**Influencing***

*Familiarity with NOC Operational Level Agreements--**Influencing***

*Ability to manipulate data on the NOC portal--**Influencing***

*Manage network bandwidth/availability and capacity--**Resourcing***

*Alt route circuits and services—**Action or Resourcing***

*Document network outages in ticket tracking system--**Action***

*Ability to use Network Monitoring Tools--**Action***

*Ability to access routers on the networks and correct anomalies--**Action***

*Ability to access switches on the networks and correct anomalies--**Action***

*Ability to access cryptographic equipment on the networks and correct anomalies--**Action***

   *Sub-task--Manage via Encryption Manager Software--**Action***

*Ability to research site information using existing NOC database--**Influencing***

*Able to make daily network health checks--**Action***

   *Sub-task--Able to ping/trace route network components to test connectivity—**Action***

With the above in place and the prior knowledge gained of the ITIL processes, the next step is to align the task categories to the applicable ITIL processes. Those without a background in ITIL may find it necessary to review the previous sections on the ITIL processes.

Task Categories Aligned to ITIL Processes

Using the Task category definitions and the knowledge of the ITIL processes both can be aligned. This requires a fundamental understanding of the ITIL processes as was previously discussed. With an understanding of the ITIL processes and the category descriptions both can be linked together. In the DISA NOC case, the result should resemble the following:

Resource

Capacity Mgt

Availability Mgt

Application Mgt

Demand Mgt

Technical Mgt

Action

Incident Mgt/service desk

Problem Mgt

Event Mgt

Change Mgt

Release & Deployment Mgt

Request Fulfillment

Access Mgt

Service Asset & Configuration Mgt

Underpinning

Financial Mgt

IT Service Continuity Mgt

Service Portfolio Mgt

Information Security Mgt

Supplier Mgt

Influencing

Service Level Mgt

Service Catalog Mgt

Knowledge Mgt

Service Improvement

Assessment of Critical Tasks to ITIL processes

With the critical tasks identified, and each assigned to a task category, and categories linked to the ITIL processes; we can now use this data to answer the fundamental problem. Which ITIL process(s) when implemented has the greatest probability of providing the agency the greatest return on their investment?

For the DISA NOC case, if the Task categories are assessed, it is determined that 9 critical tasks are Action tasks, 5 tasks are Influencing, 3 Resourcing, and one Underpinning. This reveals that the vast majority of the DISA NOC's critical tasks are Action Tasks. Knowing this, the focus on which ITIL process can be narrowed to the processes that are aligned to the Action Tasks. This provides the DISA leadership with a narrower focus on which ITIL process may be best to implement within the NOC and will provide the best benefit to the NOC and DISA as a whole. Other processes aligned to the Influencing, Resourcing, and Underpinning will not be considered (at least not initially) because the potential benefit is not justified based on the critical tasks being performed by the NOC.

DISA leadership's task of choosing a process to implement has now become easier. Incident management can be chosen if better management of incidents within the organization is need by the NOC. If the organization is involved in numerous changes that could impact the stability of the organization's infrastructure, this would also be a viable option. The key point in this methodology is that now the organization has data to guide their implementation decisions.

Results and Conclusions

Most U. S. government agency leaders have all understood that ITIL best practice could infuse efficiencies and cost savings into their organizations. This is of particular importance now is a struggling world economy where federal budget cuts and cost reduction measures are the norm and not the exception. However, for the U. S. government agency, in nearly all cases the mission isn't reduced to account for the limited financial resources, but rather leaders must seek out more efficient ways of doing the same mission as before. Doing more with less is a challenge, but ITIL when implemented within the organization properly for the agency can produce efficiencies and cost savings by standardizing processes and procedures.

The benefit and drawback to ITIL is that there is freedom in its implementation. This is of little comfort to the agency head as they struggle with decisions as to which processes within ITIL might produce the greatest benefit to the agency. Efforts were made throughout this work to explain the ITIL V3 lifecycle process to include details of all processes and functions. Unless some training in ITIL is experienced, most are unaware of the vast number of processes addressed in ITIL's systematic approach to the delivery of quality IT services. For this reason, the functions and processes were explained within the context of each phase of the lifecycle.

As revealed in the literature review, there is some generic ITIL implementation guidance available and published, but little attention has been made to the government agency needs especially in these economic times of reduced federal dollars to spend to conduct essentially the same mission. ITIL's promise to help bridge that gap comes with a challenge—where to start and how to get the greatest bang for the buck. The argument was made that although little or no ITIL implementation guidance exists for government agency leaders to use, there is a methodology that can aid these leaders in their ITIL implementation decisions once they have an understanding of the lifecycle phases and processes.

Agency leaders must fully understand their organizational mission and the critical tasks required to accomplish that mission. Understanding that these tasks are accomplished by their employees based on the established employee training plans is critical to ITIL implementation success. Once the critical tasks are identified, categorized, and aligned to the ITIL processes, the resulting data can be used by the agency leaders to make an informed decision on the ITIL process, when incorporated into the agency business processes, would yield the greatest benefit.

The importance of this research is to illustrate that although ITIL prescribes no implementation guidance, the U. S. government agency can use a methodology to provide some guidance on ITIL implementation decisions for the agency decision-makers.

References

Adams, S. (2009). *ITIL V3 Foundations Handbook.* London: The Stationery Office.

Albrecht, K. (1988). *At America's Service.* Homewood, IL: Dow Jones-Irwin.

Aligning the Drivers of High Performance. (2012, October 14). Retrieved from Mindtools: http://www.mindtools.com/pages/article/newSTR_95.htm

Baschab, J., Piot, J., & Carr, N. (2007). *The Executive's Guide to Information Technology.* Hoboken: John Wiley & Sons.

Bellinger, G., Castro, D., & Mills, A. (2012, September 1). *System Thinking.* Retrieved from Data, Information, Knowledge, and Wisdom: http://www.systems-thinking.org/dikw/dikw.htm

Bergeron, B. (2003). *Essentials of Knowledge Management.* Hoboken: John Wiley & Sons.

Bhardwah, P. (2009, November 25). *You Can't Improve it, if You are not Measureing it.* Retrieved from Not Just ITSM: http://notjustitsm.wordpress.com/category/frameworks-and-service-models/itil/

Bhatti, J. (2012). *Service Strategy Jawaid Bhatti.* Retrieved from Jawaid Bhatti: London: http://www.jawaidbhatti.com/node/44

Brewster, E., Griffiths, R., Lawes, A., & Sansbury, J. (2010). *IT Service Management: A Guide for ITIL V3 Foundation Exam Candidates.* Retrieved

September   6,   2012,   from   Books   24/7:
http://common.books24x7.com/toc.aspx?bookid=41309

Cannon, D., & Wheeldon, D. (2007). *Service Operation.* London: The Stationery Office.

Casassa Mont, M., Beres, Y., Pym, D., & Shiu, S. (2010). *Economics of Identity and Access Management: a Case Study on Enterprise.* Retrieved from Hewlett-Packard Labs, Bristol, UK:

http://www.hpl.hp.com/techreports/2010/HPL-2010-12.pdf

Case, G., & Spalding, G. (2007). *Continual Service Improvement.* London: The Stationery Office.

Cator-Steel, A., & Toleman, M. (2007, July 3-6). *The Role of Universities in IT Service Management Education.* Retrieved from USQ ePrints: http://eprints.usq.edu.au/2969/1/Cater-Steel_Toleman_Pacis_2007.pdf

DISA Vision and Mission. (2012, October 15). Retrieved from Defense Information Systems Agency (DISA): www.disa.gov

Dugmore, J., & Taylor, S. (2008, March). *ITIL V3 and ISO/IEC 20000.* Retrieved fromwww.itsmf.it:
http://www.itsmf.it/documenti/Documenti/International%20WP/ITIL_and_I SO_20000_March08.pdf

Duncker, C. (2006, July 31). *Five Business Benefits of Employee Training Programs.*   Retrieved   from   Submityourarticle.com: http://articles.submityourarticle.com/five-business-benefits-of-employee-training-programmes-7892

England, R. (2007, December 31). *A Completely Unauthorized Biography - Part I: A History of ITIL.* Retrieved June 8, 2012, from ITSM Watch: www.itsmwatch.com

Evergreen Systems. (2006). Developing the Business Value of ITIL.

Fry, M. (2010). *ITIL Lite: A Roadmap to Full or Partial ITIL Implementation.* London: The Stationary Office.

Heathfield, S. (2012). *Train Employees to Train Co-workers.* Retrieved from About.com:
http://humanresources.about.com/od/managementtips/qt/train_emp_t3.htm

Hiles, A. (2010). *The Definitive Handbook of Business Continuity Management.* West Sussex: John Wiley & Sons.

Iqbal, M., & Nieves, M. (2007). *Service Stategy.* London: The Stationery Office.

ITIL Service Level Management Software. (2012, August 17). Retrieved from Axios Systems: Service Desk and IT Service Management Software: http://www.axiossystems.com/en/solutions/itil/service-level-management.html

ITIL V3 Certification Scheme. (2012). Retrieved September 19, 2012, from Mountainview:
http://www.mountainview.ca/Mountainview/itilV3certification.htm

ITSM toolkits & templates & eLearning. (2012, August 19). Retrieved from My Commerce: Digital   River: http://www.shareit.com/product.html?cart=1&productid=300263945&affilia teid=200094437

Klosterboer, L. (2009). *Implementing ITIL Change and Release Management.* Upper Saddle River: IBM Press.

Lacy, S., & MacFarlane, I. (2007). *Service Transition.* London: The Stationery Office.

Learn ITIL V3: Key activities in Change Management. (2012, August 27). Retrieved from Learn ITIL V3: http://learnitilv3.blogspot.com/2012/03/key-activities-in-change-management.html

Lewis, K., & Schwartz, L. (2009, January 19). A Case for ITIL Return on Investment (ROI)--White Paper. Ft. Lauderdale, Florida, United States of America: ITSM Academy.

Lloyd, V., & Rudd, C. (2007). *Service Design.* London: The Stationery Office.

Oliveira, P. C. (2009, July). The Value of ITIL. Retrieved June 12, 2012, from

http://web.ist.utl.pt/ist13948/alunos/teses-2008/teses/Tese-Pedro-Oliveira.pdf

OPM Training Policy Handbook. (2007, May 11). Retrieved from U. S. Office of Personnel   Management: http://www.opm.gov/hrd/lead/pubs/handbook/sitemap.asp.

Petti, R. (2012). Introduction to ITIL. *IT Service Management 2012* (p. 17). Las Vegas: Pink Elephant.

Pollard, C., & Cater-Steel, A. (2009). JUSTIFICATIONS, STRATEGIES AND CRITICAL SUCCESS FACTORS IN SUCCESSFUL ITIL IMPLEMENTATIONS IN U.S. AND AUSTRALIAN COMPANIES: AN EXPLORATORY

STUDY. *Information Systems Management.*

Rasa, G., Kumar, S., & Wahida Banu, R. (2010, December). Release and Deployment Mangement using ITIL. *Global Journal of Computer Science and Technology*, pp. 2-8.

Reboucas, R., Sauve, J., Maura, A., & Bartolini, C. (2007). A Decison Support Tool to Optimize Scheduling of IT Changes. *IFIP/IEEE International Symposium on Integrated Network Management* (p. 10). Munich: IFIP/IEEE.

Schiesser, R. (2010). *IT Systems Management.* New York: Prentice Hall.

Syntel. (2012). *Application Management Strategic & Consultancy Service.* Retrieved August 7, 2012, from Welcome to Syntel Online: http://www.syntelinc.com/Solutions.aspx?id=327

Taylor, S., & Macfarlane, I. (2005). *ITIL Small Scale Implementation.* London: The Stationary Office.

Tiong, C., Cater-Steel, A., & Tan, W.-G. (2009). Measuring Return on Investment from Implementing ITIL. In A. Cator-Steel, *Information Technology Governance and Service Management: Frameworks and Adaptions* (pp. 408-422). London: IGI Global.

van Bon, J., de Jong, A., Kolthof, A., Pieper, M., Tjassing, R., van der Veen, A., & Verheijen, T. (2008). *A Management Guide: Continual Service Improvement based on ITIL V3.* Hogeweg: Van Haren Publications.

van Bon, J., de Jong, A., Kolthof, A., Pieper, M., Tjassing, R., van der Veen, A., & Verheijen, T. (2008). *A Management Guide: Service Design based on ITIL V3.* Hogeweg: Van Haren Publications.

van Bon, J., de Jong, A., Kolthof, A., Pieper, M., Tjassing, R., van der Veen, A., & Verheijen, T. (2008). *A Management Guide: Service Operation based on ITIL V3*. Hogeweg: Van Haren Publications.

van Bon, J., de Jong, A., Kolthof, A., Pieper, M., Tjassing, R., van der Veen, A., & Verheijen, T. (2008). *A Management Guide: Service Strategy based on ITIL V3*. Hogeweg: Van Haren Publications.

van Bon, J., de Jong, A., Kolthof, A., Pieper, M., Tjassing, R., van der Veen, A., & Verheijen, T. (2008). *A Management Guide: Service Transition based on ITIL V3*. Hogeweg: Van Haren Publications.

Wallhoff, J. (2004). *Combining ITIL with COBIT and 17799*. Retrieved from Scillani Information AB: www.scillani.com

Wan, J., & Liang, L. (2012, February). *Risk Management of IT Service Management Project Implementation with Killer Assumptions*. doi:10.4236/ti.2012.31007

Wikipedia the free encyclopedia. (2012, September 20). Retrieved from Wikipedia: http://en.wikipedia.org/wiki/Expert

Zwetsloot, G. (2003, May 3). From Management Systems to Corporate Responsibility. *Journal of Business Ethics*, pp. 201-202.

Appendix

1972	IBM starts research on quality service delivery called information Systems Management Architecture (ISMA).
1980	IBM publishes Volume I of the IBM Management series titled "A management System for the Information Business", first public edition of ISMA.
1986	UK Government agency Central Computer and Telecoms Agency (CCTA) authorizes a program to develop a common set of operational guidance with the objective of increasing efficiencies in Government IT.
1988	The Government Infrastructure Management Method (GITMM) is formalized and issued as guidelines for Government IT operations in the UK focused on Service Level Management. In the same year, the development team was expanded and work continued on Cost, Capacity, and Availability Management.
1989	GITMM title is considered to be inadequate. GITMM is renamed ITIL. First ITIL book published: Service Level Management, then Help Desk (incorporating the concepts of Incident Management), Contingency Planning, and Change Management.
1990	Problem Management, Configuration Management, and Cost Management for IT Services books published.
1991	Software Control & Distribution book published.
1992	Availability Management book published.
1997	Customer focused update to the Service Level Management book. IT Service Management Forum (itSMF) UK is chartered based on ITIMF.
2000	Service Support V2 book published. BS15000 ITIL aligned standard published.
2001	Service Delivery V2 book published. CCTA became a part of the Office of Government Commerce (OGC).
2002	Three books published: Application Management; Planning to Implement IT Service Management; and ICT Infrastructure Management. BS15000 service management standard is significantly revised.
2003	Software Asset Management book published.
2004	Business Perspective: The IS View on Delivering Services to the Business book published.
2005	International standard ISO/IEC 20000 published based on BS15000.
2006	ITIL Glossary V2 published.
2007	ITIL V3 five core books published.

Figure A1: Historical ITIL Highlights (Cator-Steel & Toleman, 2007).

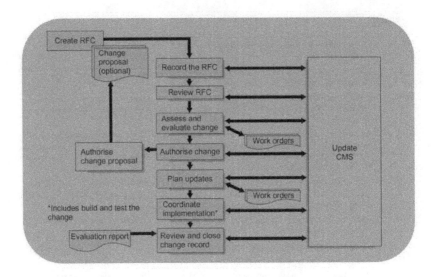

Figure A2: Change Management Activity Guide (Learn ITIL V3: Key activities in Change Management, 2012).

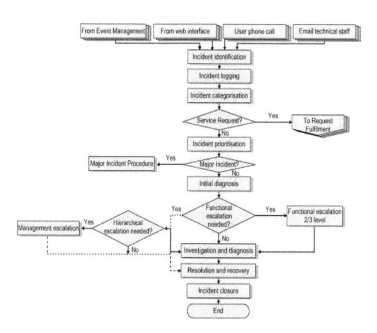

Figure A3:   Incident Management Flowchart (Brewster, Griffiths, Lawes, & Sansbury, 2010).

Government Employees Training Act (GETA)	Title 5 United States Code Chapter 41	Executive Orders (E.O.)	Title 5 Code of Federal Regulations Parts 410 and 412
The *Government Employees Training Act*, passed in 1958, created the framework for agencies to plan, develop, establish, implement, evaluate, and fund training and development programs designed to improve the quality and performance of the workforce. GETA was codified into Title 5 United States Code Chapter 41. GETA has been amended many times since 1958, including by the Federal Workforce Restructuring Act of 1994.	The United States Code is a codification (information that is ordered systematically) of those sections of legislative acts that prescribe action by Federal agencies. Laws (Acts) are codified shortly after their passage by Congress and published in the appropriate title to the United States Code. Title 5 United States Code, is dedicated to human resource issues. It is organized into various chapter headings, with Chapter 41 addressing "Training" in the Federal service.	Executive Orders provide agency heads with additional presidential direction on how the law is to be used. E.O. 11348 (1967) provides agency heads and the U.S. Office of Personnel Management with additional information on how GETA is to be carried out. It was amended by E.O. 12107 (1978). The order emphasizes the importance of using effective interagency training programs to meet common needs across Government and requires that employees be selected equitably for training.	The CFR is a codification of the general and permanent rules published in the *Federal Register* by the executive departments and agencies of the Federal Government. Title 5 CFR Part 410 addresses the general and specific policies and requirements for training in Government agencies. Title 5 CFR Part 412 addresses executive, management, and supervisory development. NOTE: Both Parts 410 and 412 of 5 CFR were substantially amended in 1996.

Figure A4: Summary of Legal Foundation of Training (OPM Training Policy Handbook, 2007).

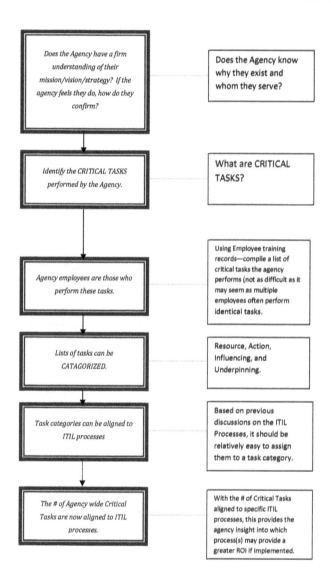

Figure A5: Mapping Agency Critical Tasks to ITIL Processes

www.ingramcontent.com/pod-product-compliance
Lightning Source LLC
LaVergne TN
LVHW042338060326
832902LV00006B/253